How to Invest in Condominiums

How to Invest in Condominiums

The Low-Risk Option
for Long-Term Cash Flow

Andris Virsnieks

JOHN WILEY & SONS, INC.

Library of Congress Cataloging-in-Publication Data:

Virsnieks, Andris, 1943–
     How to invest in condominiums: the low-risk option for long-term cash flow / Andris Virsnieks.
        p. cm.
     Includes index.
     ISBN 0-471-15150-5 (pbk.)
     1. Real estate investment—United States. 2. Condominiums—United States. 3. Rental housing—United States. I. Title.

     HD255.V57 2001
     332.63'243—dc21

                                                                                    2001026750.

Printed in the United States of America

10   9   8   7   6   5   4   3   2   1

To Jessica, my wife and best friend of many years.

Acknowledgments

I would like to thank Elizabeth Lyon and Claudia McCormick for all the help they provided in the support of my book proposal.

I would also like to thank Mike Hamilton, senior editor at John Wiley & Sons, for championing my work, and Mark Pennucci, my property manager, for reading my manuscript early on and providing positive feedback and encouragement.

Contents

Preface

The idea for my book started with a letter to Riga, Latvia. I was writing to some relatives in Latvia who had regained ownership of an 86-year-old apartment building containing 25 small apartments. They were now trying to cope with the burdens of ownership in a country that had been ravaged by a half-century of colonialism and communism. In the letter, in an attempt to provide some advice, I started to write for the first time about what I had learned from being a landlord for the past 20 years. I felt I was qualified to give some good advice because my investment in income-producing real estate had indeed yielded a superior amount of money over the years.

I had to start writing from scratch. I did not have a written investment plan, or anything else in writing, about how my real estate investments work. Whatever method or approach I was employing had evolved informally over many years. The method was so simple that there had been no need to write it down. I could remember what I needed to know and had to do. Who needs written procedures for himself on how to buy and rent out a few condominiums?

In the past, when someone at work asked me how I invest in condominiums and I only had a minute or two to answer, I would say something like: "I buy new condominiums that are selling well and then rent them out for a profit." But now I had to think about what I had been doing for the last 20 years and boil it down to information that would be useful to the new landlords in Riga. My letter, I thought, would be worthwhile if it could provide even one tip that might help them avoid just one costly mistake. I wrote that the ultimate objective of any investment is to end up with much, much, more cash than you started out with and that real estate is generally a long-term investment that won't be over until everything is sold and all the cash is collected. As an example, I pointed out that even though my rental units have been successful so far, the final results of my investment will be realized only when I sell them and collect all the proceeds. I wanted to make sure they were aware of the fact that as long as your investment is out there earning profits for you, it is subject to some kind of risk. Bad luck or good luck could alter the results before it is over. But in the short run, I wrote, they should strive to achieve the obvious goal of having the incoming rents cover all their expenses, including taxes, as soon as possible. In black and white, I told them that they should not feed those old apartments with cash indefinitely.

I wrote to them that certain skills are required to deal with tenants effectively; however, I was not current in these skills because I had not dealt with any tenants since 1981, when I gave away that big task to professional property managers. I recommended the use of expert help, and I provided some concrete examples where assistance from professionals made a big, positive difference in my real estate activities.

As I was writing this letter, I felt I could go on and on and write a long, detailed description of my approach to real estate investing. But, I also realized that the most important part of my method—purchasing of the right kind of property—could not be applied in Riga. I remembered that I had already looked into doing so in Riga in 1995. I did not get very far.

My method requires certain conditions not found in all locations.

In Riga, I had looked at an apartment building located fairly close to the center of the city. It was being privatized and had just about everything wrong with it except location. It had burnt-out elevators; floors with enough slope on them to make a ball roll; loose wiring; and broken stairs, windows, and doors. Sullen people were still occupying these apartments, which were still decorated with Soviet memorabilia, including models of ICBMs and bombers. They were not happy to have their place looked over by potential new landlords. The real estate agents showing us around were trying to sell these apartments unit by unit. At the same time, without moving the tenants out, they said, they were going to "fix up" the building. I asked if they had estimated how much all that would cost. They said there was no estimate but that everything would become clear once they started the work. This, I realized, was the extreme opposite of the kind of investment situation to which I had become accustomed. How could anyone invest in chaos like this and hope to get their money back, let alone make a profit? Only a crazy cowboy who knew how to operate in chaos would place a bet here.

I became more aware than ever before that I knew only how to invest in places that basically had nothing wrong with them. A new Western-style condominium, I finally discovered by asking around, was being built in Riga. After a long walk from the city center, we found it. The location did not look too good to us. The project itself was still in the early stages of construction. Also, when we were at the site, all construction activities seemed to have stopped, and I don't think it was a weekend or a holiday. I talked to the developer of this project, who was also a member of Latvia's parliament (at that time, no conflict-of-interest laws made this illegal), about buying one of the units as an investment, but he was not able to talk concretely about completion dates or firm prices.

Upon completing this letter of advice on how to invest in real estate, it dawned on me that if I did go on and on—given enough time—it could turn into something as long as a book.

That was an exciting idea. I had never done anything like that before. So I did go on and on, and I turned the letter into this book. But the advice therein is presently only applicable to a place that has a well-developed, diversified, and growing economy; a place not subject to boom and bust economic cycles (for example, a town in Alaska entirely dependent on oil revenue); a place where there is an orderly but free real estate market not constrained by rent control; and most importantly, a place where nice new condominium projects are being built and successfully sold to happy homeowners. These conditions exist in numerous robust cities in North America and hopefully will also exist in the near future in Latvia, the original target of my advice.

Introduction

The risk of investing in rental condominiums is about the same as investing money in your own home. The method of investing is simple and easy to apply with minimal effort, yet you can average a 21% to 26% annual return on your investment. What could be better than that? Could it be the stock market? No, it cannot, because the long-term average return for stocks is 9% to 10%. This investment works for you when the stock market is good and continues to work for you when the market is bad. Most of the time, in fact, it tends to give you a fairly stable income, such as you might get from a second job (but you won't have a second job) or an investment in bonds. But unlike bonds, this investment will not be devastated by inflation or rising interest rates. To get a wonderful investment like this, you do not send your money off somewhere far away. You keep your money close to home. You put it into hard assets on Main Street in the form of a few, simple, income-producing condominiums.

Why condominiums? Condominiums are the simplest and easiest way (I am not saying there is easy money here—a down payment, time, and patience are required to get started) to make a direct investment in income-producing real estate. And carefully selected income-producing real estate can provide you with another stream of income at very low risk to the capital you invest. This stream of income will be, for all practical purposes, immune from the rampages on Wall Street. In your rental condominium you will not encounter and be frightened by the raging bulls and growling bears that seem to populate the stock market. The condominium bylaws may permit cats, but you should never see a "dead-cat bounce" in one of your condominium rental units like the ones so often seen on Wall Street (an upward spike in a falling stock market to lure the investor in before the stock market goes into a free fall). The cash flow from good rental condominiums is so steady and reliable that if you have to think in terms of animals, a cash cow would be a much more appropriate metaphor.

An investment in a few good rental condominiums will give you protection from inflation in the short run as well as the long run and also provide some shelter from taxes. With this investment you won't have to watch the news every day and worry about losing 20% to 40% of your assets quite suddenly. You won't get any wild rides, and you will sleep well with your investment. It is quite possible to go through a lifetime of investing in condominiums, as described in this book, without ever losing any money. Every one of my condominiums is a money maker. Some are better than others, but there are no losers. I cannot say this about my investments in stocks or limited partnerships. Also, I don't personally know of anyone who has lost money investing in a few condominiums like this. But I do know lots of people who have lost money in stocks and limited partnerships investing in real estate.

I took a look at the contents of another book on investments and saw that it was going to narrow down your choice of investments to certificates of deposit, money market funds, U.S. treasury bills, bonds, municipal bonds, zero coupon bonds, and whole life insurance. My book, in contrast, is very narrow minded; it offers only one choice—investing in individual condominiums for income and appreciation. It is the first investment I found that I felt safe with as a beginner, and I was able to jump in with both feet without any fear of losing my shirt. Other investments are discussed for comparison purposes because all investments do compete with each other and condominiums, like any other investment, should be continually measured against other investment opportunities. Also, sooner or later you will have to find some other safe place for the earnings from the condominiums if you stop expanding into more of them.

This book does not attempt to tell you how to attain the right attitude toward money or how to think properly about wealth. No, this book is a call to action to make money in one, simple, single-minded way. You will get the right attitude when you see the results of your action. The initial action you have to take, however, is not difficult, unusual, heroic, or risky. All you have to do is buy a carefree, inexpensive condominium in which to live to start the action. In the investment world, just thinking and reading about investments is not enough; if you do not take action to implement an effective, long-range plan to counter the inevitable ravages of inflation and taxation, you will lose. All the analysis (which is just thinking hard about something) in the world won't help you if you don't act. You have everything to lose—not just your gains but your savings, too.

To apply the method described in this book, you do not have to have the drive, ability, knowledge, and skill of a real estate mogul. You don't have to be a natural-born wheeler and dealer because you will have to make just a few straightforward real estate purchases. And if need be, you can get a real estate broker who is on your side to assist you in making these acquisitions. You do have to have the wherewithal and common sense to buy one condominium that you would like to live in, or could live in, if you had to. That is what it takes to get started on applying this method. No brilliant entrepreneurial skills or financial skills are required. Also, luck does not play a big role. If the right condominiums are selected and properly managed, superior results can be achieved. To get these results, you will have to scout out and arrange for the purchase of a few condominiums, but from then on it will be an *investment* because your real estate broker or property manager will deal with all the other headaches. This book tells you how not to do most of the work that landlords normally do.

Most books on investing in real estate tend to cover the waterfront; they are so comprehensive that they educate you about real estate but don't really tell you what to do specifically to actually get going on an investment. Many other books are detailed and complex descriptions of how to buy and work on fixer-upper apartments or houses, and that can be a real turn-off to someone who is not ready to work very hard physically and mentally for a long time. And even this may not be enough if you don't have or do not first obtain the required skills and knowledge. This book, in contrast, is about buying and renting out new or mint-condition condominiums (no fixing up whatsoever is a requirement) for steady cash flow over a long time period. The process is relatively simple. The expected results are quite predictable, and monitoring these results is not hard work.

This book is not about learning the details of filling out an earnest money agreement or how to arrange for financing or condominium laws; I have always relied upon brokers, bankers, and if need be, lawyers for all that. But if you want to gain some expertise in these areas, plenty of books cover them in great detail. In my book I focus on the keys to success. The main key to success will not come from getting a slightly lower interest rate or paying a little bit less in real estate commissions. This is not to say that you should not shop around for the best deal. The key to success will be buying well-located condominiums at low enough prices so that you get high enough rents to provide a solid positive cash flow immediately when you decide to rent them out.

Condominiums are not immune to the laws of economics, but this process is the closest thing to a pat formula for making money in real estate that I have been able to find. A lot of people are doing this without the help of a how-to book because it is an obvious, low-risk way to make money. People in certain situations are simply compelled or naturally led to making money this way. A person who moves out of his or her condominium for some reason and decides to rent it out instead of selling becomes a direct investor in income-producing real estate. This is a safe, sane way of investing. There is a clear-cut method to this sanity that can be documented and analyzed. Written guidance can be provided for those who follow this road. This guidance will help you avoid some potholes and have a smoother trip.

From my experience I know that just a few more condominium moves like that, properly planned and executed, can make a big difference. In fact, a handful of rental condominiums can make *all* the difference. In my case, my investments in half a dozen condominiums made early retirement possible. If I had relied only on stocks and bonds—I'll never know for sure—I suspect I would still be dreaming about retirement.

So if you don't want to wait until you naturally drift into this method of investing in real estate as I and many others have done but want to get started sooner—time is money—you may find some parts of this book worthwhile. By *worthwhile,* I don't mean that you might just find parts of this book interesting but that it may actually help you invest in a condominium that gives you a return as good as, or better than, my best-performing condominiums. In the long run, you can expect to make more money than the average investor in Wall Street, especially after the long-anticipated bear market eats into the value of the stock market.

Chapter 1

Not a Bear or a Bull, but Always a Cash Cow

You Invest—The Condominiums Work

The goal of this book's method is to give you as much work to do as a passive investor, such as a stock shareholder or an almost-silent limited partner, while having the control and earnings of a successful small business owner. The basic concept is to buy a few extra condominium homes in excellent condition and rent them out for profit. It is a direct investment in real estate but does not require the knowledge or work that an investment in a duplex or single-family home would. The structure of the condominium investment allows you to leave the devilish routine details to someone else. You don't have to become a real estate expert. You have only to get to know—really well—the value of the few specific condominiums in which you decide to invest. Anyone who has rented a place to live already has some of the background knowledge required for evaluating the value of a condominium that is ready for immediate occupation by a tenant or an owner.

Controls Like a Small Business

In some aspects, rental condominiums are like a small business because they have revenue, expenses, a bottom line, and customers. In addition, when you own a rental condominium, you have some direct control that gives you a chance to influence results. You can select the property managers and check their performance. You can raise or lower the rents if need be. But unlike having a small business, there is almost no risk of failure. The failure rate in the first three years of operation for small businesses is huge (about five out of six). I am not even aware of a failure rate for rental condominiums, but if one exists somewhere, I'd bet it is tiny.

The work that a rental condominium requires, once properly set up, is one-tenth of 1% of what many small businesses require. For your condominium business/investment, you should never have to sacrifice a holiday or a weekend. How many restaurant (restaurants have the highest failure rate) or store owners could say that? I read about a woman who owns three bookstores and is so busy she cannot ever go on vacation. But she is her own boss. In your condominium rental business, you will also be your own boss, but you will be a much gentler and kinder boss.

REALITY CHECK—THE CHECK IS IN THE MAIL EVERY MONTH

My only regular contact with my five rental condominiums is a check that does indeed come to me in the mail every month. It is for the net proceeds from rents and is like a second paycheck, except that the amount varies a little bit because of property taxes and an occasional vacancy or repair bill. Getting a check like that once a month does not have the excitement of watching a hot stock move on Wall Street on a daily basis. Market psychology is lacking. Both the bulls and the bears seem to be missing. But if someone put a gun to my head and forced me to describe my condominium investments using the animal terminology of Wall Street, I guess I could let my imagination run wild. I could say that when the rental income check amount is more than I expected, I feel a little bullish about my condominiums, and when it is a little less, I might feel briefly bearish about them. At the end of the year, however, when I look back at the total results, they invariably look like a cash cow.

Now that I have been able to retire early, mainly due to the condominiums, that check from my property manager seems more like a second retirement check. Like my real retirement check, it also comes in once a month, and I also look to see if it comes in with the correct amount at the right time. But there are some differences between the two. The amounts on the retirement checks are less variable, and they come to me as direct deposits to my bank. There is nothing I can do to make the rental income checks as predictable as a retirement check from the government, but to save even more time, I could arrange to have the rental income checks deposited directly into the bank as well. But I do not intend to do this because a check in the mail is a good way of keeping me in contact with the results of my investment in my business every month. It is difficult to ignore a check you have to personally process. The amount of the check by itself already gives me an indication of how well I am doing. Success is measured one check at a time, once a month.

LOW TECH, HIGHER PROFITS

My business operations don't require the use of a computer. Using a computerized spreadsheet, for example, would not increase profits (the way to increase profits is to excel at picking the right condominiums at the start) but would merely be an additional expense. The only work I normally now do is to review the simple income statements that are included with the check from my property manager. To make this review, I enter the data the old-fashioned way, using pencil and paper, into a manual spreadsheet. Even this, however, is not essential. You can "just say 'no!'" to bookkeeping. The income statements could be just examined and then saved in a shoe box, until the end of the year, to give to your tax accountant. In earlier years I used this shoe box shortcut for quite a while to save time on monthly bookkeeping. The price for saving this time was to lose more detail into how each condominium was performing month to month.

GOOD HOURS (0.66 HOURS PER MONTH) . . .

But to take the shortcut, you must really hate bookkeeping, because the long way around, doing the manual spreadsheet, turns out not to be very long. For the purposes of this book, I now time my manual spreadsheet efforts on a regular basis, and I now know that I spend an average of about forty minutes each month doing this. Only once in a while do I have to call my property manager to clarify something. This is objective evidence that my rental condominiums are not a first or second job but primarily an investment in real estate—unlike the case with motels, which are primarily business and only secondarily an investment in real estate. And the condominiums have been the solid foundation of my investment portfolio for a long time. If you are a workaholic and you need 16 hours of work a day, you may not find this approach satisfying.

. . . BUT YOU CAN APPLY YOURSELF FOR LONGER HOURS

This does not mean that investing in condominiums is not flexible. A workaholic could make them fit his style. By learning to do everything himself, he could manage the property as a one-man show. He could do the cleaning, repairing, and painting. He could attend all the condominium association meetings. He could get elected to positions on the boards of more than one condominium. Being the president or treasurer for a couple of condominiums would help keep him quite busy. Any spare time left over could probably be easily absorbed by the career he is having on the side. The method in this book, however, is antiworkaholic—to do as little as possible, all by yourself. You want to be free of the work but not the earnings.

BOOK VALUE RISK

Carefully selected rental condominiums are less risky and will probably provide a better return than the stock market in the long run. A little more work is involved in the acquisition and setup phase than what I imagine most people do when they invest in the stock market. But this extra effort up front is worth it because it allows you to feel secure about your investment. To feel as secure in the stock market as I do about my investment in my condominiums, I would have to be able to buy into the stock market at close to book value. The last time that was possible was 1974.

FEELS LIKE A BOND

When it is properly set up, your portfolio of condominiums should feel somewhat like an investment in bonds. Well-established rental condominiums should tend to give you a relatively steady return that is similar to the regular payments you get from a bond (the return from rental condominiums, of course, is not actually guaranteed, as the interest payment is for a bond), but they also provide protection from inflation as well as shelter from income taxes and have the potential for price appreciation in excess of inflation. You receive a check every month, and all you have to do is make sure it is for the correct amount (unlike a bond payment, the condominium checks are a little different every month). It's almost like clipping bond coupons, except that with a condominium you can expect to get back all the money you invested and then still have a chance for a really big gain on top of that.

YOUR CONDOMINIUMS MAY BE WITH YOU FOREVER

If we ever have a return of a go-go era in real estate values, such as we had in the 1970s, I will be in a position to reap windfall profits. The potential for such profits, due to condominium prices blasting higher in the 1970s, is what initially attracted me to condominiums. However, to realize windfall profits, I would have to sell some of my condominiums. This would be tough to do because I have now become hooked on the monthly cash flow. But who knows, some future favorable change in the law on capital gains taxes, in combination with another boom in real estate prices, could make one or two sales irresistible.

ATTAIN INVESTMENT HARMONY

So if you invest in a half-dozen carefully selected rental condominiums now, will you have $1,000,000 in 20 years? It is possible, but nobody knows the answer to that, for sure— just as no one knows for sure what $1,000,000 will be worth 20 years from now. A million dollars already does not seem worth that much today compared with what it did 20 or 30 years ago. It is true that even today disposing of a million dollars in a year or two would still feel like an awful lot of spending for most people. But if you look at it as a source of income, a million dollars today may not even make you feel rich, let alone filthy rich. At a money market rate of 5%, $1,000,000 would give you an annual income of $50,000 before taxes. And in 1998 a lot of people who do not consider themselves rich are making more than $50,000 just from their job. Thirty years ago, roughly speaking, a person with a fairly good income might have had to work five years to earn more income than what a million dollars would earn. The future value of the almighty dollar cannot be guaranteed, and neither can the results of any investment. But once you have your income condominiums in place, it is entirely possible that you may not have to make any decisions or choices for the life of the investment, say, the next 30 years.

You can to a large degree be free of everlasting agitation and uncertainty about your investments. By remaining in your area of expertise, condominiums, you will minimize the unknowns, leave very little to chance, and get maximum results for a minimum of effort.

Chapter 2

Seven Easy Condominiums

How I Discovered Condominiums

In 1972 I bought a small old house for $10,000 because I needed a place to live. I had to use borrowed money to make this purchase, but I thought that making the $72 monthly payment to the bank to ultimately own the house made more sense than paying rent.

While living in the little house, I learned about repairs, yard work, rose bushes, watering grass, and weeds. And then weeding the weeds. I soon realized that hacking foliage was not for me. It took time away from all the other things I was doing. I also learned that real estate could be a good investment. I sold the house three years later for $13,800. A few more years after that I could have sold it for about $30,000. Isn't hindsight a wonderful thing?

Because neither renting an apartment nor living in a house was acceptable to me, I was inevitably led to condominiums as the answer to my need for shelter. Here was a place where I could enjoy looking at gardens without feeling guilty about not gardening. I suspect other condominium dwellers have chosen to live in condominiums for similar reasons (this is not to imply that condominiums are mainly a haven for anti-gardeners).

Condominium Number 1: Solid Urban High-Rise

I purchased my first condominium in 1975 for a price of $31,900 as my new place of residence. In buying it, I did wonder whether a price of $31,900 for a relatively small, brand-new, one-bedroom condominium was too high, because I was selling a small house for less than half the price. It took some time and quite a few visits to see how sales were going before I could finally make up my mind to buy into this high-rise building. The way I determined that this price was not way out of line was to add up all the monthly payments (mortgage plus taxes and condominium dues) that I would have to make to live there and then compared that total payment with the rent I would have to pay for an apartment that was about as good as the condominium.

This comparison of payment to rents was the main consideration, but I had also looked at a few other condominiums and knew that the price was competitive. I did not figure out in great detail whether I could make any money if I rented it out, but in effect I was approximating a calculation like that. I quickly made the final decision to buy when I learned that the less expensive units in which I was interested were selling out rapidly. The higher-priced units on the upper floors took a much longer time to sell. As a result of this, I later heard, the developer may have lost money on the project.

I bought my new condominium home with a 10% down payment on a 9% fixed rate conventional mortgage. The monthly installment payments were $231. Taxes were $25 a month. The owner's association maintenance assessment was $32 a month.

I lived there until November 1981, when I decided to go overseas on business. By now I already had experience renting five other condominiums successfully, so I made some calculations and decided to rent out my condominium home of six years as well. The starting rent was $415, but the condominium fee and property taxes had by now increased to $54 and $37 a month, respectively. Because I could not manage my rentals from overseas, I was compelled to get a real estate management company to do it for me. This was one of the best decisions that circumstances ever forced upon me. The management agreement required me to pay the property manager 10% of the rent, or $41.15, a month, for their service. This still left me with a small profit. The first tenant in my first condominium stayed for more than ten years, paying a steadily increasing rent. The tenant moved out only after I turned down her unsolicited offer to buy the place at the current market price.

Before I paid off the balance of the mortgage in 1992, the net income, $1,774, from rent was giving me a 55.6% return on my investment.[1] This rate of return was so high because it was calculated on only my part of the investment, about $3,190 (my down payment). Now that I have paid off the loan balance amount and don't have leverage any more, the rate of return from net rental income has been averaging about 10.5% a year.[2] But the net income and cash flow in terms of total dollars since 1993 has been much higher because I don't have to make mortgage payments anymore. This means that in 1993 I had decided it is better to make 10.5% on $31,900 without using borrowed money than making 55.6% on $3,190 with the use of borrowed money. I gave up the benefits of leverage for lower risk.

Total operating expenses for Number 1 have averaged about 47% of the collected rent. Additional expenses for repairs, maintenance, advertising, and insurance coverage (extended from my homeowner policy) have stayed quite low. As a result of this, I have already gotten back—in the form of net income after taxes—more than all the money I invested in this condominium and then some. The returns would be greater if I included the interest I have earned on this accumulated net income. But because I did not set up a separate bank account for my condominiums, I don't have an accurate figure for the interest earned on the earnings of each condominium.

Number 1 has appreciated to a value of about $119,000, an increase of about 273.0%.[3] The final results of this investment if I were to sell it would be very good indeed, even after all the capital gains taxes I would have to pay. But I continue to let it trot along at a real 10.5% return from rents.[4] On top of that, there is some tax shelter from depreciation. Including appreciation, which has averaged about 11.9% a year, I estimate I have been getting a return of 22.4% (by adding the 10.5% real gain from rental income to the 11.9% potential gain from price appreciation).[5]

As of April 1997 this condominium project was mostly owner occupied. There were 21 rental units out of a total of 135 units. This means that 16% of the condominium units were occupied by renters.

An income statement on how this unit performed in actual fact in 1997 is provided in the following chart:

Rent	$7,500
Property taxes	1,018
Condominium fee	2,256
Management	655
Insurance	87
Repairs	189
Maintenance	251
Carpet	
Paint	11
Administrative	8
Total operating expenses	4,475
Net operating income	$3,025

My calculations of the performance of my five condominiums end with the year 1997; by stopping at this year, I stay with a more conservative rate of return on investment of 20.8%. In the years 1998 to 2000 there has been a very rapid rate of appreciation in real estate prices in the Seattle area—some people call it a real estate boom—and my condominiums took part in these large increases in value (see Appendix L for more information about this price appreciation). If I were to include these large price increases that exceed the rate of inflation by a significant amount in my calculations, my rate of return on investment could increase to about 23% or 25%. And I have a feeling that over the long run such an increase probably cannot be sustained. There is a strong possibility that we are headed into a recession in the year 2001 or 2002. A lot of economists are talking about this possibility.

On July 7, 2001, the negative economic condition was making headlines in a number of newspapers across the country. The *Seattle Times* headline was quite clear about its outlook and it was not good: "Economic Numbers Continue to Worsen. Signs of Recovery Not Found As Service Employment Slows."[6] A recession, if it were long enough, would by all reasonable expectation ultimately cool the real estate market. Then we could once again expect real estate prices to stay flat or experience only small gains over an extended period of time. In such an economic environment the rate of return on my condominiums could very well drift back to a more realistic rate, which I think is about 21% (what my data through 1997 indicates). But if the real estate "boom" continues for many more years after 2001, my conservative expectations may start to look questionable and I will of course not be upset about the inaccuracy of my expectations.

Condominium Number 2: Large Suburban Multibuilding Development

Condominium Number 2 was the first one I bought purely as an investment in income-producing real estate property. Real estate prices were going up sharply in the 1970s. I felt I was qualified to invest in another condominium because I already lived in one and thus knew something about them. I purchased Number 2 in 1976 for a price of $23,950. To get a loan on it, I had to make a 20% down payment—rather high because it was going to be an investment and not my place of residence. The total down payment, including other costs, turned out to be $5,527. It was a conventional, 9.5% fixed-rate loan of $19,160. The monthly mortgage payment was $161.26. The condominium fee and taxes were $46 and $30 a month, respectively. The rent was $265. I rented it out for four years for a net income of $1,853—until I sold it in 1981 for $42,500, a 77.4% gain due to appreciation alone.[7] This sales price was higher than the stream of income from this property would justify because it was sold as a condominium home and not just as an income-producing apartment. When

I sold it, the percentage of units occupied by renters was probably similar to the percentage of rental units in condominium Number 3, about 27%. The overall rate of return on my original down payment, from rental income, appreciation, and interest income from installment payments, I calculated to be 45.6% a year.[8]

I remember that the process of selecting and buying this, my first rental condominium, went smoothly and quickly. My parents, I think, mentioned an advertisement about some relatively inexpensive condominiums being sold in a suburb north of Seattle. One afternoon I drove up there to take a look, but the only thing to see there was a construction site, some floor plans, and a small model of what the whole project was supposed to look like when completed. I asked the sales agent on the site how long they had been selling and how many units had already been sold. I remember being impressed by the rapid rate of sales, based on the numbers he mentioned. These numbers seemed credible because the sales agent could identify on the model the actual units that had been sold and were no longer available. From all this, I concluded, it probably would be a successful condominium complex.

The next afternoon I purchased a two-bedroom condominium from the developer's sales agent for the asking price after I found out about the expenses previously mentioned and learned (from reading the local classified advertisements and asking around) that I could probably get a rent of about $250. I estimated, based on this data, that with a little luck I could get a positive cash flow.

At this point I was a totally inexperienced landlord, but I had heard about such things as vacancy rates. I realized it meant you don't always collect all the rent you expected. I also realized that the exact amount of extra expense, whether for cleaning, painting, or repairs, was not exactly predictable. But real estate prices were going up fast, and inflation was nipping at the heels; I had to go for it. At this time, I was thinking of holding this property for a short time and then selling it for a quick gain. Little did I realize that I was drifting into a lifelong method of investing.

Now I had my first rental unit and started to learn about being a landlord by doing. I learned about how to find renters by advertising in the newspaper, a little about screening tenants, but luckily not too much about arranging for repairs, because this was a new condominium and no serious repairs were required. The rent had to be collected. The condominiums dues had to be paid on time. A minimum amount of bookkeeping was unavoidable. I had a full-time job that already left me with precious little time for all my outside interests. I was looking for a good investment, but now it seemed I had also stumbled into a part-time job.

I tried to keep down the time spent on managing my first condominium rental unit. I had the tenant send the check for the rent directly to my bank. I also paid the condominium dues three months in advance to reduce the clerical and bookkeeping effort required of me. I kept the rent a little bit lower than the market in the hope of keeping tenant turnover to a minimum. Tenant turnover means work for the landlord. Whenever possible, I got the tenants to sign a longer-term lease to keep my personal workload down. This became more and more important as I acquired more condominiums.

Now that I have sold Number 2 and have the benefit of hindsight, I can definitely say it was a great investment. But I am pretty sure I would have probably gained even more by keeping it going as a rental to this day.

CONDOMINIUM NUMBER 3: LIKE NUMBER 2 BUT IN ANOTHER SUBURB

I bought Number 3 in 1978 for $25,950. The cash down payment required for this one was $6,752, and the loan was for $19,400 at 9.5%. The monthly mortgage payment was

$170, the property tax was $39 a month, the monthly condominium fee was $44, and I was able to get a rent of $260. The process I went through deciding to buy was very similar to the process I had gone through with Number 2 two years earlier. This was a similar condominium project built by the same developer in an adjoining suburb. Again I based the decision to buy on an estimate of the income I could earn from rent and the rate at which these units were selling while still under construction. This time, however, I signed the papers after just one visit to the construction site. My positive experience with Number 2 gave me the confidence to act more quickly with Number 3.

By 1981, Number 3 was yielding better results than I had originally estimated in 1978. Amazingly enough, taxes had decreased by $10, to $29 a month, and market forces had allowed me to increase the rent by $65, to $325 a month. The condominium fee, which covers such things as grounds maintenance, water, sewage, and garbage, had increased by only $5, to $49 a month. Here also my records show that I paid these fees three months in advance to reduce my workload.

In 1992 I paid off the loan balance on Number 3 as well, but even with this loss of leverage, it continues to provide a return that pleases me. Net rental income from Number 3 is yielding on average a 13.0% return on my investment.[9] It has appreciated to about $60,000, representing a 131.2% increase in value.[10] This would amount to a 6.6% increase in price every year.[11] So roughly speaking, Number 3 has been earning about 19.6% (13.0% plus 6.6%) a year, not including the tax shelter benefit resulting from depreciation. Also, like Number 1, it has returned all of my investment and more.

As of April 1997 this condominium project was mostly owner occupied. There were 10 rental units out of a total of 37 units. This means that 27% of the condominium units are occupied by renters.

An income statement on how this unit performed in actual fact in 1997 is provided in the following chart:

Rent	$7,060
Property taxes	696
Condominium fee	1,664
Management	636
Insurance	87
Repairs	65
Maintenance	
Carpet	
Paint	
Administrative	
Total operating expenses	3,148
Net operating income	$3,912

CONDOMINIUM NUMBER 4: SMALL SINGLE BUILDING CLOSER IN

I bought Number 4 in 1979 for $27,950. The cash down payment required for this one was $5,987. The loan was for $20,963 at 11%, and the monthly mortgage payment was $200. Taxes were $27, the condominium fee was $41, and I was able to get a rent of $290. The decision process to buy was very similar to the process I went through with Numbers 2 and 3. This time, however, I made a number of visits to check out Number 4. The building had just been built; I could actually inspect it and select my unit. In spite of my inspection, the first heavy rains revealed some minor leaks, which the builder fixed. Most new buildings seem to have some bugs that have to be worked out.

As in the case of Number 3, taxes decreased! In 1981 taxes went down by $5, to $22 a month. The loan balance on this one was due in 1984, and I decided to pay it off instead of refinancing. Number 4 without leverage is providing on average a real return of 9.7% on my investment.[12] It has appreciated to about $63,000, a 125.4% increase in value.[13] This would amount to a 6.6% increase in price every year.[14] So roughly speaking, Number 4 has been earning about 16.3%

(9.7% plus 6.6%) a year, not including the tax shelter resulting from depreciation. Also, this one, like Numbers 1 and 3, has returned all of my investment.

As of April 1997 this condominium project was mostly owner occupied. There were 9 rental units out of a total of 26 units. This means that 37% of the condominium units are occupied by renters.

An income statement on how this unit performed in actual fact in 1997 is provided in the following chart:

Rent	$5,850
Property taxes	698
Condominium fee	1,200
Management	528
Insurance	87
Repairs	
Maintenance	
Carpet	
Paint	
Administrative	1
Total operating expenses	2,514
Net operating income	$3,336

CONDOMINIUM NUMBER 5: APARTMENT COMPLEX CONVERTED TO A CONDOMINIUM

In 1979 I also bought Number 5 for $19,950. The cash down payment required for this one was only about $2,000. The loan was for $17,955 at 10.25%, and the monthly mortgage payment was $162. Taxes were $18, the condominium fee was $38, and I was able to get a rent of $280. The decision to buy Number 5 was more difficult. I was moving away from what had worked out well for me so far. Number 5 was a two-year-old apartment complex, located quite a long distance south of Seattle, that had been converted to a condominium.

I remember being a little concerned that these converted condominium units were not selling very rapidly. Up until then I had been buying only brand-new condominiums that were selling well. However, income analysis for Number 5 indicated I could get a good return, assuming things went as I had come to expect. I expected Number 5 to perform about the same as the others, and I thought the price was low (only about six times the estimated gross annual rent) for a two-year-old, one-bedroom apartment with more than seven hundred square feet of space. It was also in good condition.

Things did go as expected for about five years, during which time I had only one tenant. He paid on time and was not any trouble at all. In fact, he was perfect for my management style, which could be generously called a strict form of management by exception—or more accurately described as the "I hope I don't have to do anything at all" approach to management. However, after this renter moved out, Number 5 started to show a small negative cash flow due to a higher-than-average vacancy rate and additional expenses for cleaning, painting, and repairs.

The property started to demand my attention. One time the manager for the condominium complex called me to tell me that my condominium unit was being used as a brothel because every day he saw a lot of women coming and going from the place. The real story was that my local property manager, who took care of only that unit for me, had rented my unit to a young businessman who was using it as an office from which to sell entertainment books. All those women were his telephone sales force.

I tried for a while to turn Number 5 around by finding a new local property manager, who improved cash flow a little bit for a while but not enough. Number 5 continued to be too much of an exception. It failed to help me meet my goal of not working more than one hour a month on my condominiums. I decided to get rid of Number 5.

I sold Number 5 in 1992 for $26,500. This amounts to only a 32.8% gain from appreciation after all those years.[15] But I calculated my fully realized return on investment—including the positive cash flows before 1983 and the negative cash flows thereafter—to be 26.7% a year.[16] So my most troublesome condominium rental unit did not do too badly, say, compared with an investment in a good stock mutual fund during a bull market. But I must say that Number 5 was more trouble than clipping bond coupons. I don't plan to have another one like it.

When I sold Number 5, it had a similar percentage of rental units as condominium Number 6, about 93%.

CONDOMINIUM NUMBER 6: ALSO CONVERSION, LOCATED NEAR NUMBER 5

In 1979, I also bought Number 6 for $31,000. The cash down payment required for this one was $7,750. The loan was for $23,990 at 11.5%, and the monthly mortgage payment was $231. Taxes were $27 a month, and the condominium fee was $38 a month. I was able to get a rent of $300 plus a cash-flow payment of $40 from the seller for the first 12 months. Again, as in the case of Number 5, the decision to buy Number 6 was more difficult. I was moving away from what had worked out well for me so far. Number 6 was in an older apartment complex only six miles from Number 5. It was now being converted to a condominium. And I don't remember that these converted condominium units were selling very rapidly either.

The main reasons for finally deciding to buy were that paying $31,000 for this two-bedroom apartment with more than 800 square feet of space was reasonable and that rents would likely increase at about 10% a year for the next few years.

Not only did the projections for rent increases turn out to be too high, but Number 6 has also experienced a higher-than-average vacancy rate. This in turn caused me to occasionally get involved with the on-site rental management at this project. I have been close to selling it a number of times, but each time I think about selling, Number 6 seems to settle down and produce a better cash flow. The most recent turn for the better occurred in 1997, when Number 6 managed to stay 100% occupied and generate a return of 9.8% from rental income—its best performance in five years. So I have kept it. In 1991 I had already paid off the loan balance. As a result of this, from 1993 to 1997 it yielded an average return of about 5.5%.[17] At this rate it would take about eighteen years to get all of my investment back. This condominium is returning a rate that is about the same as a money market rate, not including the tax shelter benefits from depreciation expense. The main reason for this poor performance is a high average vacancy rate (about 30% on average for the last five years— including the zero vacancy rate in 1997). If Number 6 could achieve a vacancy rate in most years like the rest of my condominiums have on average, about 4 to 6%, the return on investment could be about 10% instead of the 5.5% mentioned previously. There is plenty of room for improvement.

Number 6 has only appreciated to about $39,000, or 25.8%.[18] This amounts to only a 1.4% increase in price every year.[19] So roughly speaking, Number 6 has been earning about 6.9% (5.5% plus 1.4%) a year, not including tax shelter resulting from depreciation. If I sold it today, it would probably go down in history as my worst-performing rental unit. Many times I have thought that the only thing that could rescue Number 6 and turn it into a better investment than, say, a poor investment in bonds would be increased inflation. After the good performance in 1997, there is a small basis for hope that perhaps those more bountiful 12 months are the start of a new and more profitable trend. But that will be possible for Number 6 only if it does not give me too much more trouble and force me to sell regardless of slightly better results.

As of April 1997 this condominium project was mostly occupied by renters. There were 158 rental units out of a total of 170 units. This means that 93% of the condominium units are occupied by renters.

An income statement on how this unit performed in actual fact in 1997 is provided in the following chart:

Rent	$3,796
Property taxes	526
Condominium fee	*
Management	148
Insurance	87
Repairs	
Maintenance	
Carpet	
Paint	
Administrative	
Total operating expenses	761
Net operating income	$3,035

*The condominium fee for this unit is paid by on-site management and is already subtracted from the rent.

CONDOMINIUM NUMBER 7: SMALL ONE-BEDROOM CONVERSION BUILT OVER THE WATER

I bought Number 7 in 1983 for $79,000, which was considerably less than the asking price. The cash down payment required was $4,485. The loan was for $75,000 at 13.875%, and the monthly mortgage payment was $881. Taxes were $49 a month. In 1986 I was able to modify the loan. The new loan balance was $74,519 at 10.75%. The monthly payment for principle and interest was $704, and the monthly tax reserve payment was $80. The condominium fee was $95. Adding these last three numbers together results in a total monthly payment of $879.

From these numbers, you can see that I would have needed to get a rent of about $900 just to produce some income, let alone a positive cash flow. But I bought this unit to be my new place of residence indefinitely. I knew the price—even after I had negotiated it down—was high relative to the rent it would fetch, but this was where I wanted to live. I had looked at a lot of other places in about the same price range. I also felt, however, that because it was over-the-water property (even better than waterfront property?) and a neat place to live, Number 7 had superior price appreciation potential. It is smaller and older but has those three most important things going for it: location, location, and location.

Indefinitely, this time, turned out to be three years. I moved out of Number 7 in 1986 and rented it for $465. As expected, I got some fairly significant negative cash flows. In other words, I was losing real money on Number 7. I thought these losses would go on only for the short run, but I was not sure how long the short run would be. Over the next few years the rent increased and performance improved, especially after tax performance, because Number 7 had so much interest and depreciation expense to write off.

In 1991 we found out there is a price for being over the water. The pilings on which the building stood had to be reinforced to meet earthquake standards. At the same time the homeowners association decided to redo the whole outside of the building to solve some persistent water leak problems and improve the appearance of the place. My share of the special assessment for all this was $11,500. This, of course, was very bad for cash flow but should improve the value of the investment in the long run. I know of one condominium owner who has purchased special assessment insurance to protect herself from financial surprises. This is something you might consider to protect yourself against unexpected expenses.

In 1991 I paid off the loan balance. Ever since, Number 7 has been a basically trouble-free unit yielding a return from rent of about 3.9%.[20] This was less than the current money market interest rate in 1998. At this rate, I would get all of my investment returned to me in about 25 years.

However, Number 7 has appreciated to about $140,000. This amounts to about a 62.6% gain from appreciation, including the negative effect of the special assessment, but I do expect more significant appreciation in price in the future because it is waterfront property.[21] I realize that now I am speculating about future results. But to compare Number 7 with the other ones right now, appreciation has averaged about 4.2%, and so I estimate I have been getting a return of 8.1% (adding the 3.9% real gain from rental income to the 4.2% unrealized gain from price appreciation).[22]

As of April 1997 this condominium project was mostly owner occupied. There were 11 rental units out of total of 47 units. This means that 23% of the condominium units are occupied by renters.

An income statement on how this unit performed in actual fact in 1997 is provided in the following chart:

Rent	$8,203
Property taxes	1,058
Condominium fee	1,875
Management	679
Insurance	87
Repairs	125
Maintenance	467
Carpet	150
Paint	
Administrative	
Total operating expenses	4,441
Net operating income	$3,762

LESSONS LEARNED

1. You can see from this history of my condominiums that you do not have to do anything especially clever to apply this method. Basically all you have to do is buy new or mint-condition condominiums and rent them out for a long time. But even as simple as this investment process is, it can be improved with the benefit of hindsight.

Looking back, it is now easy to see things I could have done differently that would have increased profits. Applying some of these benefits to the future could help increase condominium profitability by about 5% (how I calculate this potential increase in profits is provided a little later on). A 5% increase in profits could make a big difference over 30 years.

2. The most important lesson learned was not to buy into projects that will be occupied mostly by renters. From my experience, the rents tend to be lower, the vacancy rate is higher, and the appreciation in price, as a result, is lower. This was the case with one of the conversions I sold and remains the case with one I still have. The rule for the future should be to buy into condominiums in mint condition that are already mostly owner occupied or newly built condominiums that are selling well, mostly to people who will live there.

3. Conversions as a rule should be avoided, unless there is something special about some project that convinces you that it will be a successful conversion. The percentage of rental units in my least successful condominium (Number 6), a conversion, is a whopping 93%, and the return on investment is only 6.9%. There seems to be a relationship here between conversions, a high percentage of rentals, and lower return on your money. But for my special waterfront condominium (Number 7), also a conversion, the percentage of rentals in the building is only 23%, and the return on investment is only 8.1%. If the 8.1% return improves, this conversion will prove to be a good exception to the rule. It will prove that, given enough time, a super location can overwhelm the negative attributes of being a conversion—sometimes.

4. The average percentage of rentals for my condominiums (calculated by using the percentage of rental units provided for each condominium project earlier in this chapter), excluding the two existing conversions, is 25%; including these conversions, it's 36%. And if all conversions

are also excluded from my calculations of my return on investment, it would increase from 20.8% to 26.0%.[23] This means that if I had simply refused to buy any condominiums that had previously been apartments, my rate of profit would have improved by 5.2% (26.0% minus 20.8%).

5. By buying additional units in one really good condominium complex, you do reduce diversification. But this additional risk would have been worth taking because good units are not easy to find, and the additional gains from cash flow would have been worth the extra risk.

6. Don't change the game plan to chase after gains or yields that are too good to be true. You know what they say about returns that are too good to be true. Keep trying to find condominiums that are the same or similar to your successful ones. Stay within the area of your expertise. If you come across a condominium that will give you an unusually high yield, you should look at it twice as hard before you buy. Extremely good numbers should be interpreted as a warning signal that something else might be extremely wrong. If you find a $100,000 condominium that can be rented out for $2,000 a month while all the other $100,000 condominiums you looked at will rent for only $1,000 a month, you must uncover the reason for this. You must find out why the rent is so high or why the price is so low. Does the building have a serious structural problem that has not been disclosed? Is something very bad, like a garbage dump, to be constructed nearby? Are the numbers wrong? Or could it be that the seller is naive or just plain generous?

7. Also, I should have learned earlier than I did that the missing ingredient in my condominium investment concept was *professional management*. This has made all the difference. The investment can carry on by itself most of the time. No special endurance is required from me to stay with it for the long run. To maintain this efficiency, you should try to avoid having more than one

property manager to deal with for all of your condominiums.

I think I successfully applied most of these lessons to the last condominium we purchased, in 1986, as our place of residence. We have no plans to rent it, but if we did, I expect it would yield a positive cash flow with or without the leverage we once had (in 1997 we paid off the mortgage). It has also appreciated by about 50% (and this occurred during a period when real estate in Seattle had been statistically flat). This indicates that the right condominiums can continue to provide superior returns in the future.

How have my condominiums performed compared with other rental condominiums? Based on informal discussions with other investors in income-producing condominiums, my general impression is that they have experienced, on average, results that are similar to mine. There is no guarantee that you will experience results like this in the future. You may do better. You may do worse. But this brief history is indicative of what you might experience in the next 20 years.

Chapter 3

Principles for Selecting the Right Condominiums

One Move Can Make You a Landlord (in Name Only)

A common way for many people to become condominium landlords is to rent out the condominium in which they have been living when they move on to live somewhere else. In a situation like this, the decision to rent can be based on a high level of knowledge and understanding about your investment, because you have lived in your investment. You should know what it costs to live there and would probably have an idea if the place has been going up in value. You are in a very good position to know if your condominium home is worth keeping and renting out.

I think that this is the best way, at least when starting out, to acquire good rental condominiums slowly and carefully. In my description of the process, I will assume that you can make all the necessary moves to achieve the ideal results. In doing this, we will derive the very best rules and guidelines.

If You Cannot Beat Them, Join Them

Say that you are an apartment dweller who loves living in apartments but you wake up one morning with a not-so-brilliant realization that collecting rent would be better than paying rent forever and ever. This realization is so strong that it becomes a goal you are ready to go after, patiently but persistently, as long as it is profitable. After a little thought, you see that the most conservative way to move toward this goal is to first stop paying rent and after that work on the problem of collecting rent. To stop paying rent, you have to buy a place to live in. And with your preference for hassle-free apartment-style living, you are inevitably led to buying a condominium.

SHOP AROUND A LOT

Buying a condominium is the most important step in the process. So at this point you should spend some time shopping around for the best buy and asking a lot of questions about cost, size, number of rooms, storage, and parking space. In this way you will get a good, practical education about condominiums.

You should look at more than a dozen condominiums to find one in which you would like to live and can afford. To stay on the conservative side, you should try to find one where it will not cost you significantly more to live on a monthly basis than the apartment you have been renting. If you are not sure what you can afford because this is the first time you are buying real estate, you can ask a number of bankers if they would give you a loan to buy the condominium of your choice. They will help you figure out if you can afford to buy the place. By going to several bankers, you will increase your chance of getting the best conventional loan the market has to offer at the time. Also, you should look to your real estate broker to help you get a loan that is favorable to you. The beginning of this investment program is just learning how to get a place in which to live that belongs to you. You have to establish a solid base camp on the mountain before you can climb higher and set up the next camp.

AVOID OBVIOUS FLAWS

Before buying into an already established condominium building or complex, find out what the bylaws say about rental units. Also read the minutes of a number of condominium owners' association meetings to see if there are any serious problems you may not want to live with. You should look for a condominium in mint condition that has mostly owners living there. Just like other resident owners, you want the number of rental units to be limited.

Too many rental units in a given condominium could have a negative effect on resale prices. As a general rule, you should not buy into a condominium that has more than 30% of the units occupied by renters. I did not pull this figure out of thin air; there is a little research behind it. I called a large condominium management company and got from them the data on the number of rental units in their various condominium projects. From this data I calculated that 29.4% (calculating by each condominium project, the figure would be 21.5%) of the total condominium units they managed were occupied by renters.[1] I called another management company, and they said that a 30% rental rate was also about the average they were experiencing for their condominium projects. (In Chapter 2 you saw that I have experienced a similar average number of rental units in my projects: 36% rentals for all of my condominiums and 25% rentals if conversions are excluded from the calculation.) They also said that if the percentage of renters starts going too much higher than 30%, property values may start to be adversely affected, and if it goes over 50% renter occupied, values may start going downhill fast. There seems to be a good explanation for why this happens. In July 1997, I called a large financial institution that is a big lender of money to condominium buyers, and they said that they require a condominium project to be 60% owner occupied for them to make loans in that project. If people cannot borrow money to buy into a condominium project, the effective demand for units in that project is bound to be reduced, and thus its value will suffer. If banks don't like to put money into condominium projects with too many renters, neither should you. Bankers know that the return *of* their money is more important than the return *on* their money. You should have the same kind of priority.

In Chapter 2, I demonstrated how I could have improved my rate of profit from 20.8% to 26.0% if I had not invested in condominium projects where a high percentage of units are occupied by renters. Had I avoided a few of these condominiums by establishing an ironclad rule against investing in conversion projects (some with an owner occupancy rate as low as 7%), the average percentage of renter-occupied units for my condominium investments would have been pushed down to 25% from what it actually is, 36%. This indicates that you can generally improve the quality of your portfolio by investing in condominium projects that are mostly owner occupied. But, of course, there is no guarantee that an increase in the percentage of owner-occupied units in a project will automatically cause an increase in the rate of profit for all rental units in that project.

In addition, a high turnover rate for rental units could affect your investment's value. By talking to local residents and the on-site manager (if there is one), you should be able to find out if the renters in the complex tend to stay for a long time or if there is a lot of turnover. If the latter is the case, this could be an indication that something is wrong with the place—a serious "don't buy signal" that you may want to heed. Like the other owners, you want to own a condominium home that will keep up in value.

You should check to see if any large special assessments are to be expected. You do not want to be surprised by any large bills you have to pay all of a sudden. In some condominiums, the regular monthly homeowner dues are relatively low owing to their practice of paying for large repair bills with special assessments. In other condominiums, the homeowner dues may be relatively high because the extra money collected is used to build up adequate reserves to take care of significant repair bills without resorting to a special assessment.

You should also, of course, make a physical inspection of the whole condominium to make sure you are not buying someplace with totally inadequate storage space or a terribly tight parking spot. And don't forget to verify that the place actually has the number of square feet of space that you were counting on having in your new residence.

ARE THEY SELLING LIKE HOTCAKES?

Before buying into a brand-new condominium, you want to make sure that it will be a successful, mostly owner-occupied project. To do this, you should make sure that the project is selling at a fairly rapid rate. A new 120-unit condominium in Whistler, British Columbia, sold out within an hour.[2] To work as an investment, your condominium does not have to be red-hot like the one at Whistler, but for a project with about a hundred units, for example, the developer's sales agent should be able to prove to your satisfaction that he is selling about ten units a month. You want to find a place that gives every indication that it is in the process of being sold out successfully as expected by the developer.

If you have difficulty selecting the right condominium to buy, you might consider hiring a broker to help you. At this most important step, the expense of professional help could be worth it. But if after doing your own analysis and getting advice from professional real estate people, you are still not sure about buying a particular condominium, don't buy; watch and wait until you are sure. There may be a price to pay for waiting longer and buying later, but that is a risk worth taking if it prevents you from ending up in a half-empty condominium that then degenerates to a de facto apartment building. I was not sure about my first condominium. I had my eye on a unit on the fifth floor that was going to cost $29,100. I looked at it a couple of times, but I did not buy right away because I was not sure if the project was selling fast enough. I continued to look at other condominiums, and weeks later I came back to see how things were going. Everything was sold out at the project up to the eighth floor. I quickly bought a unit on the ninth floor for $31,900. By watching and waiting a little longer, I was pushed up four floors, and at a price increase of $700 a floor, I had to pay an extra $2,800. But that was the price of being certain that I was buying into a building that promised to be a going concern as a condominium for mostly resident homeowners. If I had waited still longer, I would have been left with a choice of more expensive units located at an even greater altitude. This waiting game, of course, would not work with hot projects such as the one I mentioned in Whistler; before you could figure out the sales rate, the game would be over, and you would have to look for another condominium project.

It Is Not Enough That You Like It and Can Afford It

Remember that now you have an ulterior motive. Once you have found the condominium you can afford and in which you want to live, do not make the final decision to buy until you also figure out how profitable or unprofitable it would be to rent out. That means you have to take all the monthly payments you would have to make, add them up, and then subtract that amount from what the rent would be. The result will be an estimate of the cash flow, positive or negative, that you can expect to see every month.

Estimate Expenses

The payments that you will have to make will be the mortgage, condominium fee, property taxes, a rental management fee (if you decide to let someone else take care of all of the details, as I so strongly recommend), and other expenses such as maintenance, repairs, insurance, and advertising. The amount of the first three payments can be obtained from the bank and the real estate agent, and they will have to be paid regardless of whether you or a tenant lives there. The rental management fee will be about 9% of the rent. The other expenses, from my experience, will average about 7% of the rent.

Estimate Rent

The most accurate way to estimate what the rent will be would be to find another unit in the building or complex that is already being rented and is the same or very similar to the unit you want to buy and then ask the tenant or owner how much the rent is. If that is not possible, you must find out the rents for apartments or other condominiums nearby. The best way to do this is to actually take a look at a couple of places close by and ask what the rent is. By doing this, you not only get the information you need to make your calculations but also have an opportunity to size up the competition. As well, you should look at advertisements for rentals to get a general idea of the level of rents in the area. Or you can estimate what a condominium's rent might be the easy way: Simply ask a property manager who is actively managing condominium units like the one that interests you.

INCOME PROPERTY?
ONLY IF THE PRICE IS RIGHT

Now, assuming you have gathered all this information, you are ready to make the calculation that will tell you if the price you are ready to pay for your new home is reasonable from an income-producing point of view. Using data from a real live condominium, I provide a detailed calculation in Appendix A. You should make a similar calculation. Sure, it may be generally true that a home is a good investment, but you want solid, quantified proof that your *particular* investment will actually produce money.

You have heard the simple and oh-so-true formula for making money: Buy low, sell high. When investing in income-producing condominiums, you have to buy low enough and then rent them out high enough to get a good return from the rent alone. If you buy a piece of income-producing property that meets all these requirements, you will probably also be able to sell it for a higher price someday when you want or need to. Rental income and price are closely related. Over time, both will usually be pushed up by the forces of supply and demand.

In the long run, you should end up buying low and selling high. You should have to rely on only very long-term trends continuing, and you should not buy expecting to do this in the short run. The greater fool theory may not work for you. Rapid inflation may not be there for you at the right time to rescue you from your mistake. If you do not buy low enough, you may be stuck with loss property rather than income property for a very long time.

CAN YOU MAKE (OR LOSE) MONEY—IN YOUR HEAD

After you make this calculation and do a little analysis, you will see that the monthly rent has to be more than 1% of the price of the condominium you are about to buy if you are to have any chance of renting it out for a profit. This means, if the price of the condominium is $100,000, you should get a rent of $1,000 or more a month. This is only to be used as a rule of thumb to quickly size up the reasonableness of the asking price. Also, you can quickly determine without the use of a calculator what the return would be on your investment if you bought the place for $100,000 cash (great, forget the mortgage). To do this, you make the conservative assumption that 50% of the $1,000 rent will be eaten up every month by expenses and that you will get to keep only $500. This means you could earn $6,000 a year, or 6%, on your $100,000 investment. All this just tells you quickly that the price and the rent are somewhere in the right ballpark.

So if you were ever determined to buy a wonderful $200,000 condominium that would command a rent of only $1,000 a month, you would know that you are paying about two times too much. The price-and-rent relationship for this otherwise excellent condominium would be about two blocks away from the ballpark. If you had to rent it any time soon, you would have to feed this condominium with large amounts of cold, hard cash every month. Nevertheless, if you kept this expensive condominium long enough, even it might become a viable rental unit someday. An overpayment of 100% is bound to cause financial bleeding, but time may heal some wounds, sometimes. If we assume you need a rent of about $2,000 a month for it to be a going concern and further assume that the rent will be increasing at 6% a year, we can calculate what *any time soon* or *long enough* means as follows: The rule of 72 allows us to easily calculate, by dividing the 6% rate of increase into 72, that a 6% compounded rate of increase in rent would take 12 years to double the rent to $2,000 a month. So after bearing all the expenses of holding onto the property for 12 years, you could only then start hoping to break even.

BEFORE YOU GET SERIOUS, USE A CALCULATOR

Clearly the $200,000 condominium with a rent of $1,000 is not a good investment idea. The $100,000 condominium has possibilities, but more calculation is required, because if you bought this condominium and set rent for it at $1,000, you would be violating another rule of thumb that is more frequently used to buy income-producing real estate: Never buy any real estate for more than seven times the gross annual rent. To buy a $100,000 condominium under this rule, you would need a gross annual rent of $14,286, which is calculated by dividing the price of the condominium ($100,000) by seven. This means the monthly rent would have to be $1,190 (the gross annual rent of $14,286 divided by 12 months). And $1,190 is 1.19% of $100,000 ($1,190 divided by $100,000 multiplied by 100%), which means that if you used the 1% rule of thumb to buy, you would pay too much! To be really on the safe side, you should mark up the result you get from the 1% rule by 20%.

Another way of looking at it is that if you bought a $100,000 condominium and got a monthly rent that was 1%

of the price, you would have bought it for 8.3 times the gross annual rent. The gross annual rent would be $12,000 (1% of $100,000 multiplied by 12 months). The 8.3 is then calculated by dividing the gross annual rent ($12,000) into the price ($100,000). To get the 8.3 down to 7 or to get the 1% up to 1.19%, you have to either get a lower price or a higher rent.

These kinds of calculations are important, but numbers alone are not enough. I once bought into an apartment, through a limited partnership, that had great numbers. The price was only five times the gross annual rent. In spite of such strong numbers, the partnership was not a success. I saw the numbers, but I never saw the property myself (let alone lived in the property for a while, as the best rules on condominiumism recommend). Price and rent numbers by themselves don't give you a balanced evaluation of income property. An evaluation of the quality of the property is lacking.

WHEN WILL THE CASH FLOW?

Now assume you want to buy the condominium represented by the data in Appendix A. Should you buy this condominium and move in? Appendix A shows that at a price of $94,400 and rent of $1,000 a month, with a zero vacancy rate, the cash flow would be negative by $46. Every month, if everything went about as expected, you would have to find at least $46 somewhere else to make up the difference between the rent and all the payments you have to make.

To start getting a positive cash flow, the rent would have to increase by about 10%, to about $1,100 a month. Appendix B shows you the difference that a 10% increase in rent makes. Keeping everything else the same, you would now have a positive cash flow of $45 a month.

From past experience as a renter and after a little research, let us say you decide that a 10% increase in four or five years is a reasonable expectation. This does not mean that you will be faced with a real-life situation exactly like the one depicted in Appendix B, because over four or five years your expenses would also have increased by some amount. But for purposes of this discussion, let us assume that it is reasonable to expect a positive cash flow situation in four or five years and you make the big decision to buy the place.

SOMETIMES YOU CAN NEGOTIATE TOO HARD

When buying the place, you should, of course, try to buy it for less than the asking price. If a project is selling well, however, this may not be possible. I paid the asking price for all the condominium units I purchased in brand-new projects. If you do decide to try to negotiate a lower price, don't lose sight of the main objective in the process—making a lot of money in the long run. About twenty years ago, I offered to buy a two-bedroom condominium on the shore of a lake for about $40,000. The asking price was about $42,000. My offer was rejected, and I did not make another. I can only guess at the amount of rental income I am missing now. But I do know that that particular condominium is still there and is well kept up—it's now worth about $230,000. However, in our example you do not miss out on making the purchase by trying to shave a few percentage points off the price. You pay the full price, $94,400, and the sale is closed smoothly and quickly. With this method of investing in real estate, you don't have to go around making numerous ridiculous offers.

NOW, AT LAST, TIME IS YOUR FRIEND

The hard part, buying your first condominium, is over; now just enjoy it. You have escaped from the clutches of your landlord. You don't have to pay rent anymore, but you do have monthly costs that come to $886 (taxes, $123; condominium fee, $151; and mortgage, $612). This amount may or may not be higher than the rent you were paying before, which would mainly depend upon the kind of apartment in which you were living previously. Your total monthly cost should increase gradually, as property taxes go up and condominium fees are raised. You just make these payments and get to be an expert on your condominium simply by living there. You keep up with what is going on by reading the minutes from home-owner meetings or even by attending some of these meetings. You participate in all elections and vote on everything, even if just by proxy. You wait for the forces of supply and demand and inflation to increase the general level of rents in your area.

Now let us assume that your expectations are realized. After a few years, rents for condominium units like yours have gone up to where you can get a positive cash flow. You decide to go to the next step and collect some rent as well. To rent out the place where you are living, obviously you will have to find another place to live. The classic solution to this problem would be to buy another condominium, repeating the process you went through a few years earlier—except that you would be doing it better, because you have experience now. You are now really on the way to building wealth, one condominium at a time.

RENTING IT OUT IS NOT YOUR JOB—DELEGATE

Once you have bought and moved into your second condo-minium, you are ready to rent out your first one. This is easy to do because you don't actually do it yourself. You hand this task, along with the keys to your old place, to a good property manager. For about 9% of the rent that is actually collected, your property manager's responsibilities will be to find and keep desirable tenants, set and collect rents, pay condominium fees, pay property taxes, minimize vacancies, maintain your property, and make evictions if necessary. Your main role will be to check the statement or report from the property manager and to deposit the rent money in the bank every month. For my five rental condominiums, that task usually requires 40 minutes of my undivided attention every month. I am sure that many people spend more time reviewing their investments in stocks or even their bank statement. However, this is not to suggest that you can treat your condominiums in exactly the same way as money in the bank. You should have more to do with your condominiums than just review statements about them from your management. It is in your self-interest to act as a good steward of your property, and this means that you should check on your condominiums yourself once in a while. You should make sure with your own eyes that your property is being properly maintained. For me, a quick inspection of one of my condominiums docs not scem very arduous. I usually find inspecting work to be easier than doing work (I realize that a full-time professional inspector may not agree with this).

I know someone who rents out his condominiums and does it all by himself. Many times when he has to deal with some problems, he starts talking about selling. I don't encounter such hassles, because property management takes care of most of them without my assistance. By doing it all yourself, you could end up selling your property—for the wrong reason at the wrong time—due to needless frustration with the property. Also, I suspect that most people who try to manage all by themselves do not keep track of their time and don't pay themselves a decent hourly wage. They do not calculate the real total cost of doing business. They may be fooling themselves by overstating the real return on their investment.

But you could also be made to feel foolish if you hand over your property to the wrong people to manage. When I said that it is easy to rent out your place I made a big and important assumption: I assumed you already knew a *good* property manager. If you don't, you have to find one by shopping around. This is your second most important task after finding good condominiums. If you find a competent property manager the first time, you may never have to do it again. This book is all about doing only the essential work yourself and giving away the rest to someone else—but finding the right people to do your work for you is something that you *should* do yourself. In other words, your goal is to outsource everything except your core competency, which can be narrowed down to counting the money and selecting the right condominium and property manager.

You can select the right property manager by getting to know a few of them and then comparing them with each other. But how do you select the few property managers you might want to look at more closely? One way is to go to the yellow pages in the telephone book and make a list of property managers located fairly close to your rental condominiums. You can then narrow this list down to a few candidates by conducting brief telephone interviews. Or it might be easier and quicker to make a short list of property managers based on recommendations from people experienced in dealing with income-producing property (for example, landlords and property management firms). Don't be surprised if they recommend themselves, because many property management companies handle both condominium projects and rental real estate property. By going through the yellow pages or by asking for recommendations, you should be able to select a few property managers who are good enough to interview.

Once you have narrowed down your list of property management candidates to two or three, the next step is to ask each one of them to give you a formal management proposal, including a management contract. Before you conduct your interviews, you should carefully read and compare the proposals that the various companies submit to you. By comparing the management proposals and then later interviewing the various property managers, you should get satisfactory answers to the following questions:

1. How much will their property management service cost?
2. What other fees are there, such as advertising fees, renewal fees, setup fees, and so on?

3. How long will the management contract last?
4. How much experience does the property manager have?
5. Is it mainly a property management company, or does it primarily sell real estate?
6. How will they keep you informed? What reports will you get and how frequently?
7. How frequently and under what circumstances will the property manager visit your property?
8. Will your funds be kept in a trust fund that will be audited on a regular basis?
9. How long has the average landlord been using the services of their company?
10. Are they available 24 hours per day, seven days per week for consultation and emergencies?
11. What do they do about late payment and nonpayment of rent?
12. How will your property be advertised?
13. How will repairs to the property be taken care of promptly?
14. How do they screen new tenants? Does tenant screening normally include the verification of rental history, credit references, criminal record, and employment history?

In addition to getting satisfactory answers to all these questions, you should also check out some references. This means you should talk to a number of landlords who have been working with the property manager you are going to interview. And the landlords you select as references should not be the same ones who originally recommended the property manager to you. When you talk to these landlords, ask them if the property manager has done a good job. Has the vacancy rate been kept as low as possible? Have profits been maximized?

If you go through all these steps properly, you should be quite certain about which property manager will serve you best. You ought not to flip a coin on such an important choice.

THE BUCKS STOP HERE

Delegating most of your work requires some initial effort on your part, but after considering all the ramifications of the do-it-all-yourself option, you will realize how much more preferable it is to simply check reports from your property manager. Doing so may not take very long and may not be very difficult, but it is an important routine activity that you should perform carefully. By checking these reports, you will actually be monitoring the performance of your first rental condominium on a monthly basis. The amount of the checks you receive will clearly tell you how your first one is doing in comparison to your expectations.

If, as expected during the next two or three years, you have an increasing positive cash flow, the property goes up in value, and you are a landlord in name only because no significant problems require your direct involvement—then you may want to consider expanding. In most situations, the decision to expand should be based on how well your first rental condominium is actually doing in terms of cash flow. You will also probably want to take into consideration how much it might be appreciating in value. And last but not least, you may not want to buy another condominium if the first one felt more like a big hassle than a good investment.

How much of a return you should be getting from cash flow and appreciation to justify buying another condominium at this point should be based on comparing this investment result with other possible investments. If you are not getting a better return than 10%, you probably should not go on to rental number two, because a long-term investment in a conservative stock mutual fund could probably do as well (assuming you can hold on to it long enough while it fluctuates). "Nine to ten percent a year is the generic long-term return for stocks, the historic market average."[3] If you can do just as well by merely holding on to some stocks or stock funds and getting average results, why go to that extra bit of trouble that is required to acquire rental condominiums? You should not have to "buy" diversification away from Wall Street by sacrificing the return on your investment. You should expect your condominiums to beat the stock market by about 5% and relatively smoothly, without all the jarring ups and downs.

WILL YOU MOVE FOR MORE

But to move on, let us assume that your first condominium is giving you superior results: Are you ready to move again to buy another condominium? If you are, then you know what to do. You repeat the process. If you do not want to move again but want to get another condominium to rent, you can try to buy one and then rent it out right away. In doing this, you should be just as careful in selecting the property as if you were going to live in it. I have found that it is difficult to practice what I am preaching here. I always spent more time looking for the condominiums I was going to live in than the ones I was going to rent out directly. For not always practicing what I preach, the rate of return on my investments has suffered.

Buying a quality place is the most important aspect of the process. You don't want to buy a run-of-the-mill, apartment-like unit that is only pretending to be a condominium. Your choice should have something special about it. By looking at a lot of projects, you will develop an eye for seeing through the disguise of the apartments that are being passed off as condominiums. You want to buy a condominium *home* but at a reasonable enough price that it can be rented out profitably in the near future. The condominiums you select have to have homelike qualities and be selling well at the right price. A balancing act is required, just as in so many other realms of real life.

Depending on the market for condominiums at the time, you may or may not have difficulty in buying a quality condominium and renting it out immediately for a positive cash flow. If you decide to buy such a condominium that you cannot rent out immediately for a positive cash flow, you can occupy it yourself and wait for rents to go up. The temporary negative cash flow you suffer will be absorbed or hidden in your personal living expenses. On the other hand, if you are lucky enough to find a decent condominium that can be purchased and rented out immediately for a positive cash flow, great! But before you go ahead and do this, be aware that you may lose a couple of benefits that come along with living in your investment first. The first benefit you may lose is financial. The banks usually require a larger down payment and a higher interest rate for buying property that will not be your primary residence (in my case the required down payment for buying rental property was usually as high as 20% to 25%). The second benefit you will lose is the in-depth understanding of your investment that you would get if you lived in it for a while. You will miss the opportunity to give the place a real-life test. However, I know from personal experience that you may very well miss that opportunity occasionally because to live in each condominium you buy may turn out to be too impractical for you.

Of the seven condominiums I have purchased, I lived in only two of them before renting them out. If I had put more stress on looking for homelike qualities in the units I purchased for renting out directly, I may have passed on one or two of my weaker-performing units. And if I had actually had to first live in two of my conversions, I am sure I would not have bought them. I know of a number of condominium landlords who first lived in every one of their condominium rental units, and not one of them owns a conversion. My impression is that all those rental units that were good enough to have first been occupied by the landlord him- or herself are performing really well. I would not be at all surprised that the average rate of return on their condominiums turns out to be better than mine.

The quality of the selection you make at the point of purchase will determine the amount of your cash flow for years to come. Good property management will be able to do only so much for you to offset the negative consequences of any poorly chosen units you hand over to them to manage. Remember that you can always choose to slow down and not to buy another condominium for a while.

TAKE A SHORTCUT—BUT BUY AS IF YOU WERE MOVING IN

If this method of investing in real estate is really working out well for you and you are absolutely driven to expand more rapidly, you are faced with a choice of moving more frequently or taking the speedier, less conservative path of buying condominiums for immediate rental. Without taking this shortcut—directly to the rental phase—the normal path of this investment process tends to be quite slow. You would have to move every 5 years to acquire three rental condominiums in 15 years (or every 3 years, to have five condominiums after 15 years). If this is too slow for you and you insist on going faster by buying a condominium you are not going to live in first, you should honestly ask yourself the question: "Would I really like to live there myself?" before you go ahead with your decision. Don't underestimate the importance of your seriously considered answer to that question. As I mentioned before, I am quite sure I probably would not have purchased one or two of my weaker units if I had put more stress on the importance of these kinds of questions and answers. Also, if I had asked and answered that question about some of the apartments in which I invested through limited partnerships, I might have saved some precious capital. If you have to take shortcuts, they should be carefully chosen, or you may take more time to get to the top than the long, slow way around. In focusing on these important questions and answers, however, you should not forget the requirement for a positive cash flow, and neither should you forget that a lot of other people have to like the place as well.

EXPANDING CAN BE GOOD, BUT OVEREXTENDING IS ALWAYS BAD

Regardless of how you decide to expand rapidly—whether you do it by buying and moving into a new condominium every year (this would be arduous, but a dedicated condominiumist could do it) or buying two or three rental condominiums in one fell swoop—make sure you are not overextending yourself financially at the same time. Acquiring each new condominium is like climbing out further on an exposed ridge: You should stop once in awhile in a safe place and see if you can keep climbing up with very minimal risk of falling. You should move on only when there is no fear and be so sure of the next step that you can take it with a feeling of joyful anticipation of profits. If you are overextended, I doubt that you will be able to devote only one hour a month to monitoring your investment and not worry about it the rest of the time.

ABSORB THE UNEXPECTED WITH A BUFFER

Before you expand directly into additional rental condominiums, build up your cash reserve as a bulwark against the unknowable future. Even the basic level of competition you will face in your locality for renters may not always be as predictable as you would like. Usually, past trends in the level of rents are a pretty good indication of the rent you can expect to collect in the future, but sometimes events occur that are not reflected by past trends (at least not in the short run). For example, a large apartment complex could be built unexpectedly—by a workaholic developer who also knows how to work smarter—right across the street from your newly acquired condominium. And this hardworking individual could charge rents that are lower than those contained in the data you used to guess at future rent levels. This example is not something I have ever experienced; it is merely my attempt to dream up a scenario that is plausible and hopefully scary enough to motivate you to build up a very comfortable cash buffer. With adequate cash reserves, you would be able to withstand this competitive pressure and come out a winner in the long run. The shock of lower rental income will impact your money and not your peace of mind. You can climb on up with confidence if you know you have some protection.

PLAY IT REALLY SAFE

If you are especially motivated by the fear of losing any capital, you could use the cash flow from your first rental condominium to pay off the mortgage and then, only after that, think about expanding. You could be even more conservative and think about expanding only after you have also paid off the mortgage on the condominium in which you are living. And you could still go for more safety by investing only when you can do it without using any leverage at all.

DIVERSIFY LESS, RISK MORE, AND GAIN MORE WITH MULTIPLE UNITS IN ONE BUILDING (TWO EGGS OR MORE IN ONE BASKET)?

So now let us say you are in a very strong financial position, and you definitely have the means to expand rapidly; does that automatically mean you can buy another condominium? Of course not. You have met only one requirement for expansion. Having the ability to expand is not enough. The only reason you would want to do so, no matter how much money you have, would be to buy excellent condominiums that will produce a positive cash flow and are likely to appreciate in value. Buy another condominium only if you can find one that you and a lot of other people like and all the numbers are right.

Finding investment-grade condominiums is not always easy, so when you do locate a good project, you may want to consider buying more than one unit. You may decide to do this because it looks like an opportunity that cannot be passed up. You have looked at all the other comparable projects in town, and this is the best one. By having more than one unit in a project, you will be less diversified geographically among different projects (competition from that smart workaholic apartment developer across the street would now impact more than one of your units). However, if it truly is an excellent project, it might be worth the extra risk of having more than one egg in a given basket. I have never owned more than one unit in the same condominium project. But with the benefit of hindsight, I now know that more concentration of rental units in the good condominium projects and less diversification in the weaker ones would have yielded better results.

I know of one condominium landlord who has concentrated all his rental units (about three) and his residence in one high-quality condominium building. One advantage of this approach is that he never has to move from place to place. He did not have to search far and wide to find rental units so good that he himself could live in them. All his rental units are exactly the same as or very similar to his own residence. Another advantage is that he always has firsthand and very current information about his investments. He can be like a hawk perched right on top of all his eggs, watching each one very carefully.

In this way he may be able to counter some of the risk he created by choosing not to diversify. By concentrating on one good condominium project he may ultimately get a higher return on investment than I do, assuming that nothing bad happens to the building, the community within the building, or the neighborhood in which the building is located. However, judging from the main point of view expressed in this book, this landlord has gone the wrong way. He has, in effect, taken on a job in order to try to enhance his gain. He automatically gets this job by living too close to his tenants. Perhaps one of his renters even lives right next door to him. Living right in the middle of all his investments does not enhance his freedom. It is probably next to impossible for him to avoid getting deeply involved in the inevitable details and hassles of rental property and condominium management. Even if he hired a professional property manager, the renters would always have easy access to the owner whenever anything was bothering them. Unless this landlord truly enjoys being involved in the nitty-gritty of renting his units and all the details of condominium living, he won't be happy. He will know that he is sacrificing valuable time that could be used to do more interesting things.

More Caution and Still Lower Risk

So we know that you can minimize risk by reducing debt and by getting the right amount of diversification. But still more can be done to lower risk. If you are ready to make a couple of extra moves, you can put even more caution into this investment process. These additional steps will give you a chance to take a better look before you make another big leap forward. By moving around a little bit, you can delay making the decision to buy the next condominium until you have more accurate data. When you are ready to rent out your first condominium (the one in which you have been living), you could become an apartment dweller once again. You will be paying and collecting rent at the same time; one rent will feel too high, and the other rent, too low. But you will put up with this confusion for a while to see how the first condominium actually performs before you buy another one. If you see that it is not working out as expected, you have an easier way back down the mountain. You can move back into your first condominium once again without having possibly overextended yourself. You don't want to own a second condominium when the first one is not providing an adequate positive cash flow. You have a way out of your investment by moving back into your investment. You do the right thing. When the weather gets bad, you temporarily move back down to a well-established base camp.

Being a tenant for a while also gives you the flexibility to be a more aggressive investor. For example, I once visited someone who was living in a small house that he was renting very inexpensively on the edge of town, but at the same time he owned and rented out a luxury condominium in an upscale area. To beat this guy at this game, you would have to live in a really cheap trailer or a tent (I heard about an owner of a small office building who would sneak into his own building every night to find free lodging, but for landlords of residential real estate, this is not a practical cost avoidance tactic). The price for this aggressive approach to condominium investing is your own comfort, and you don't build equity in your place of residence by paying rent—no matter how low the rent it is.

But this book is all about how to invest in condominiums, and here I am suggesting you make money by living in a cheap apartment or trailer. So here is a better idea. If you are ready to move again and like the flexibility that goes with becoming a tenant for a while again, why not rent a condominium and live in it as a tenant for while? The rent you will have to pay to live in a condominium may well be quite a bit higher, but you will get a chance to kill two birds with one stone. While you are watching and waiting to see how the cash is flowing from the condominium you are renting out to someone else, you can also check out your next possible condominium purchase up close and personal by living in it. If everything works out well—the rental condominium produces abundant positive cash flow for you, and the condominium in which you are living turns out to be worth buying—you can make another very careful step forward in your investment program without having to move your place of residence. The step forward is to stop paying rent once again and buy the condominium (the big assumption here is that the owner is willing to sell it to you for the right price). But if things don't work out, you have left yourself plenty of room for maneuvering. If the condominium you are renting out is not profitable, you can, with relative ease, move back into it as mentioned before. And if the condominium in which you are a tenant turns out not to be of investment-grade quality, you won't be stuck with it. You will have to move again, however, when you find a better prospective condominium in which to live on a rent-to-buy trial basis.

LIVE FREE AT LAST

A milestone of some significance in this investment process would be to reach the point where the cash flow from your rental condominiums would cover all the payments you have to make for the condominium that serves as your residence. Looking at Appendix C, you can see that this could probably be done with just two rental condominiums *if* you owned them outright and thus did not have to make that mortgage payment of $612 a month (see Appendixes A and B). If you owned (debt free) two rental condominiums like the one in Appendix C, your cash flow from them would be $1,132 (two times the net operating income of $566). To live in your residence, your monthly payments would be $886 (taxes, $123; condominium fee, $151; and mortgage, $612), as we calculated earlier. Now the positive cash flow from your two rental condominiums exceeds the monthly payments you have to make for your residence by $246 a month ($1,132 minus $886).

To figure out how many rental condominiums it might take for you to live free in a different situation, you will note that total operating expenses for the condominium depicted in Appendixes A and C are 43.4% of the rent. This means that 56.6% of the rent you actually collected from one debt-free rental condominium would be available to you to cover your own living expenses. For my condominiums, the total operating expense has averaged a little below 50%. This lower yield is mainly due to some of the conversions I bought. Operating expenses for apartments generally vary between 35% and 45%.

In following the most conservative path, the next thing to do would be to also pay off the mortgage on your residence before you even considered thinking about expanding. To have as a goal owning one or two debt free condominiums with large positive cash flows is a great way to make sure you don't bite off more than you can chew. But the chance for realizing bigger gains through appreciation and additional rental income is reduced because you are not expanding as rapidly as might otherwise be possible. However, many significant summits can be reached merely by patiently taking a lot of short easy steps, one at a time, step after step, to the top. And when you get to the top, you won't be bored because from your new high-altitude viewpoint you will more easily see new mountains to conquer. The next higher one might be to have enough rental condominiums to cover all your living expenses. If we assume that putting a roof over your head takes about one-third of your total annual living expenses and that two rental condominiums would cover that expense, the next really big peak clearly looms right in front of you: About four more rental condominiums, or a total of six, would cover all your living expenses. So are you now totally free? No, but you are getting mighty close. At this point you should probably still keep your job to more rapidly accumulate very comfortable cash reserves.

LIVING IN THE CONDOMINIUM IS NOT AN ABSOLUTE REQUIREMENT

This common way process I have described does not mean that people who do not live in condominiums cannot successfully invest in rental condominiums. I know of a number of people who live in single-family homes and know how to buy and rent out condominiums successfully. Some longtime apartment dwellers also own rental condominiums.

But if you are not an experienced condominium dweller and you decide to get into the condominium rental business, you should put even more emphasis on the question, "Would I like to live there myself?" And if you have been living in a suburban house with, say, 5,000 square feet of space for the last 10 years, you might change the question to "Would I have liked living there fifteen years ago, when I was, perhaps, used to less space?"

How Many Can You Have?

How many individual rental condominium units can one person manage effectively? I read about a person in Florida who had 30 units and, according to the account I read, was doing well. But it sounded like he had a full-time job managing them.

How far you go with this is up to your judgment and ability. Remember, more is not always better. If you start buying too many, you may drift into the dangerous habit of buying by the numbers alone. The quality of your condominium portfolio could deteriorate rapidly. I am holding comfortably at five. At this level, the investment risk feels about as low as if I were living in a very large house and merely renting out the extra rooms I could not use myself.

If I decide to move and hence expand to another rental, before we paid off the mortgage we would have been faced with the scenario somewhat like the one reflected in Appendix A (negative cash flow with leverage) or Appendix B (rent 10% higher than Appendix A) or somewhere in between. I know that mine is a good condominium because I have been living in it for more than 10 years. I am a member of the board of directors of the condominium association, and thus I have firsthand knowledge that the condominium is in good shape financially and physically. I know that there are only a few rentals in the building and that the turnover rates for owners and tenants are low. This is just one indicator that this method of investing can continue to produce superior results in the future.

ACCOUNTABILITY—BE FAIR TO YOUR CONDOMINIUMS

Say you have decided on your comfort level—the number of condominiums you want to have for the long run. From the very beginning, it would be a good idea to track separately for each condominium the cumulative cash flow and the cumulative interest earned on that cash flow. If you do not actually earn interest on all of the cash flow from your condominiums because you are using this cash for something else, you should then make some calculations to properly rate your condominiums' performance. You should estimate how much interest you would have earned from this surplus condominium cash, as if the money had been in a separate bank account all the time. (It might be worthwhile to set up a separate bank account for each condominium, but I have not actually tried that myself.) This way you will have a more accurate idea as to how much each condominium has contributed to your wealth. You will be better able to compare each condominium's performance with the others and to other investments that automatically reinvest their earnings (I have estimated the interest earned on the accumulated cash flow from my condominiums but have not included these gains in this book for the sake of simplicity and to be more conservative in my estimates of earnings). You would not get a fair comparison of your rental condominiums' performance to a stock mutual fund investment if the dividends from the mutual fund are automatically used to buy more shares in that mutual fund and you forgot that you bought a new car with the surplus rent money from your condominiums. If you don't take into account what your condominiums have really done for you in the past, you will have a distorted opinion of them.

The very nature of investing in real estate tends to make it a long-term process. For most people, buying a rental condominium will be a big first step that will be difficult to take. They may very well be investing money they cannot really afford to lose. Emotionally, this will be a totally different game than playing the stock market with a small amount of money that they think they can afford to do with as they will. As a result, they will look long and hard before they take that step; they will want to be as sure as possible that the footing is firm before they put their full weight on it. In addition to the relatively large amount of money that is involved, the slow drawn-out process you have to follow to buy real estate will also tend to discourage most people from buying a condominium on impulse. Most people will find it much easier to buy and sell stocks on a whim than to buy and sell a condominium. You can buy and sell stocks with just one quick call to your stockbroker. One quick call to your real estate broker will not get you a condominium, and neither can you get rid of a condominium that easily. Whether you buy a new car or not, you should have a fairly accurate opinion of each condominium, and a substantial part of their contribution, in the form of real money, should always be available in the bank. A cash reserve is necessary because real estate by its very nature lacks liquidity. If, for example, you have an unfortunate coincidence where one condominium is uncharacteristically vacant longer than expected and at the same time a special assessment must be paid on another one, you will not be upset by a temporary shortage of cash. You will not unfairly blame your condominiums or start thinking about selling. Instead, you will simply write a check against their reserve account and go on with business as usual. Your condominiums will not be an unjustified source of worry in your life. And you will always be aware of their true value, based on their total contribution over the long run.

Chapter 4

Why Condominium
Investments Succeed

You Cannot Pick Up the Phone and Buy a Condominium

My impression is that a large number of people who now believe they can make a killing in the stock market do more research and analysis when they buy a television or a car than when they buy a mutual fund. In this regard, you will find a condominium to be more like a television or a car than a mutual fund. You should do research before buying your condominium home, just as you would before buying a television or car except that you will do much more of it because a condominium is a much bigger ticket item than a television or a car. You will feel compelled to compare a lot of prices for what you get in return and make the best decision for yourself based on your needs and on what you can afford.

In contrast, if you buy a stock mutual fund, your purchase will probably be based on someone else's recommendation and on how the fund's price has been behaving recently. Most mutual funds are just too large and complicated for you to understand in the same intimate way through shopping around a lot, as you can a television, a car, or a condominium home. In addition, most people will not be starting from a base of zero knowledge when they start looking at condominiums. Almost everyone seems to have some knowledge about real estate values, apparently from just being around in this world for a while. They may not have ever thought about investing, but after a certain age, most people will have had quite extensive real estate experience under their belt. It is practically impossible to avoid learning the basics, either from paying the rent or being responsible for a mortgage. You can prove this for yourself: In a large diverse group of people, start talking about stocks and see how many blank stares you get. Then compare that response to the one you get when you say something about the general level of rents or the cost of mortgage payments.

CONDOMINIUM DISCIPLINE

If the condominium was difficult to get into and is difficult to leave, you will feel somewhat locked in and will tend to stay with your investment in a disciplined fashion for the long run, unless there is something really wrong with it—for example, a persistent negative cash flow with an unfavorable trend. If this happens, you should probably get out. By following the steps outlined in this book, a significant negative cash flow should hardly be possible. But if it does occur, it is a very serious situation, and you should not go on with any expansion plans until it is corrected. No condominiums with a persistent negative cash flow should stay in your portfolio for very long. Almost every investment advisor will tell you not to fall in love with your investment. That is good advice, and it should apply to your condominiums. Your attachment to them should be conditional, primarily on a positive cash flow.

I feel locked in enough in my condominiums that I probably would not take action to sell them even if their performance deteriorated by, say, 10%. But that locked-in feeling would not be strong enough to keep them in my portfolio if I had to feed them with cash month after month. In a free society like ours, being locked in has a negative connotation, but it will help you achieve superior results in the long run. The discipline imposed upon you by the structure of the investment will help you to stick to it in a moment of weakness. That extra little bit of self-control, if you can find a way to impose it upon yourself, can make all the difference in any field of endeavor. For example, some talented Russian pianists may not have practiced enough to fully develop their potential greatness if they had not been locked in a room with a piano. That locked-in feeling for these pianists was quite literal. The structure of the teaching method led to them practicing for long hours. To be really successful with this method of condominium investing, you have to have the discipline to stick with it for decades.

There are, however, some condominium investors for whom that locked-in feeling is really more than a feeling. They are in effect just as sequestered as those Russian pianists. I am thinking of condominium owners who are renting condominiums, because they cannot sell them without suffering a big loss. This is a more severe form of condominium discipline being imposed upon them by the marketplace. You should avoid being really locked in like that and strive to have only rental condominiums in your portfolio that you can sell, if you need to, for a gain. This is a very achievable goal, and you should not have to work very hard at it if you use the slow, careful method described in Chapter 3.

I don't think you can feel good about your condominiums if they seem to be undermining your real gains in wealth from rental income by depreciating in resale value at the same time. But some people in the condominium rental business feel that even this more severe form of condominium discipline has served them well. The man in Florida with 30 condominiums whom I mentioned earlier was forced to discover the condominium rental business because he was really locked in to his first condominium by poor real estate market conditions. And according to him, he is now happy to have been stuck with this condominium: "Fortunately for us the resale market was still bad. After an unsuccessful attempt to sell my condominium, I advertised it for rent. . . . The seasonal rentals made my payments for the year."[1] He found that his condominium was easier to rent than an apartment because of all the amenities that it had to offer. Also, he discovered he could get better financing to buy condominiums than to buy apartments.[2] For reasons like that he went on to buy condominium units 2 through 30 instead of waiting for a better resale market to get rid of condominium unit number 1, as he had originally intended.

Only time will tell how this emphasis on renting well and turning a blind eye to price appreciation will work out. Will rental income make up for a lack of price appreciation? Will the resale market for condominiums in that part of Florida turn around to make those 30 condominium units an ideal real estate investment, an investment that is providing a positive cash flow and is also appreciating in value? But what happens if circumstances compel him to sell his condominiums before the resale market turns around? As a general rule you should not intentionally step into a less-than-ideal condominium investment. Before you put another condominium out for rent, you should be as sure as you can be that you'll enjoy positive cash flow and price appreciation.

Taxing Punishment for Breach of Discipline

There are some additional and very real financial reasons for maintaining your discipline and keeping your condominiums as a long-term investment. If you have had your condominiums for a while, they have probably appreciated in value, and you have probably also been writing off depreciation to reduce your tax payments—so you know that if you sold your condominiums, you would have to pay some significant capital gains taxes. Your condominiums are sending you a very clear message: If the cash is flowing, why not defer this tax event indefinitely and continue to accumulate still more tax-sheltered income from these same old condominiums? You cannot get out. Positive cash flow has locked you in.

For example, if you had bought an income-producing condominium for $70,000 10 years ago, it had increased in price to $100,000, and you had written off $20,000 of depreciation expense during the 10 years you were renting it out, then the depreciated cost basis of the condominium would be $50,000 ($70,000 minus $20,000). Now, say, you sold it for $100,000 but actually received only $90,000 in cash because the sales commission and other selling expenses came to $10,000. Your gain for tax purposes would be about $40,000 ($90,000 minus $50,000). Suppose you had a marginal tax rate of 28%; then a rough estimate of the tax you would have to pay for making this sale is about $11,200 (28% of the $40,000 gain). The message is clear: If you don't want to pay $11,200 now, don't sell now.

In hard, liquid cash (money you can spend), your $100,000 condominium is worth about $78,800 ($90,000 minus the $11,200 tax). Notice that we are lucky enough not to have any borrowed money that we have to repay in this example. If the $78,800 could theoretically be put in a money market fund to earn the going interest rate (about 4.8% in 1996), you could earn about $3,782 in interest a year. This can be compared with the cash flow from a given $100,000 condominium. And all these hard dollars are now exposed to inflation. You will need a really good reason to go to the trouble to liquidate a good condominium.

NEVER LOSE, SAFETY FIRST; AVOID ALL BULLS, BEARS, AND HIGH EXPOSURE

I like to think that the first and most important rule of mountaineering is to never fall. With just a few investment condominiums in your portfolio, the first and most important rule should be to never, ever lose any significant capital on any of your few condominium investments. You can carry out this rule if you are just investing in a few condominiums, but it would be practically impossible to do over a lifetime of investing in stocks. Even Warren Buffet, the world's greatest investor, lost gigantic sums of money by buying certain stocks for a high price and then selling them for a lower price.

This method of investing in income-producing condominiums is very suitable for people who are afraid that if they take one really good fall, they may not be able to get up again. I heard a psychiatrist say that people value a dollar lost twice as much as a dollar gained and that people overestimate their ability to deal with losses. This could be an explanation for why financial newsletters sell better when they forecast a stock market crash or a depression. Many people need something more fail safe than the stock market for investment. In spite of the statement, repeated by so many investment advisors like a drumbeat, that stocks will give you a better return than anything else in the long run, they continue to be unsuitable for most investors. Only about 20% of investors invest in stocks in the United States, and in Germany the figure is only about 5% (these percentages were increasing during the bull market of the 1990s).

I think we have all heard stories about exceptional individuals who, in trying to start some kind of an enterprise, lose their capital or even go bankrupt a number of times. They fall down again and again, but they keep on struggling until they finally succeed big time. They keep getting up and going on until they get to the top. These stories are passed on because they are inspirational and relatively unusual. There are, however, many more stories we don't hear about as much where people with limited resources who are maybe a little less resilient have one big setback and never try again. I think we all like to believe that if we mess up in the first act, we can always come back in the second. A hopeful attitude toward life like that helps us keep going. But in reality, too many times the first act is so bad that it precludes a second act; the mess left on the stage makes it impossible to raise the curtain again. The performance is canceled. In other words, it is nonsense to think that most people can lose their life savings once or twice and then somehow bounce back and get to the top anyway.

With the don't-ever-lose approach described in this book, you should never have to find out if, or how much, you can bounce. Like a very cautious mountain climber, you will chose the route with the least exposure to the top of a small mountain of your choice.

RESPONSIBLE BUT NOT HECTIC

From a daily activity point of view, your condominiums will not make you feel like you are running a small business.

Unlike managing a successful store or a restaurant, doing so will not keep you very busy. If you are doing it correctly, you should feel the very opposite of hectic. On the other hand, you *are* a small businessowner in the sense that no one else has a share in your "company" and you have direct responsibility for all of it. You are not just going along for a wild ride or a random walk, as an investment in the stock market is viewed by some investors. This sense of responsibility is good because it, too, will help reinforce a conservative long-term approach to investing.

CONDOMINIUMS COULD RUB OFF ON YOU (CREEPING CONDOMINIUMISM)

Most of the time condominiums may be viewed more as a passive investment (like shares in a utility fund) than as a business because they are not very management intensive. But once a month when you do your bookkeeping, you have to think of your rental condominiums as a small business. Like any other business, rental condominiums also have revenues, expenses, and profits. These numbers represent an important bottom line for you to track. From this monthly practice of determining the bottom line, you will come to think and feel like a businessowner without putting in the 16-hour days. Slowly, over a longer period of time, this practice of responsibility that comes from property ownership will tend to transform your habits more effectively than reading self-help books or attending motivational lectures. The bottom-line mentality may creep into other aspects of your life; you might come under the influence of creeping condominiumism. You may drift from occasional thriftiness to outright frugality. You may amaze yourself and find other sources of cash flow in your previously untouchable budget for consumer goods. The condominiums in pure bookkeeping terms, of course, won't get any credit for this increase in your affluence.

Unlike Errol Flynn, You Will Stand by Your Principle

While owning a number of rental condominiums, it will be difficult to maintain the Errol Flynn philosophy that people who die with more than $10,000 (a modern-day Errol Flynn would probably use at least $100,000 as a guideline) to their name are failures. You will instead start to adopt the philosophy of early New Englanders, who viewed the act of dipping into principle as one of the worst things a person could do.

Whether a person is motivated by enlightened self-interest (is that the same as the sheer joy of just having some money?) or greed or by a desire to make money to help others, after watching the bottom line for a while and seeing how revenues, expenses, and available capital are intimately interrelated, he or she will be loath to dip into principle. The condominiums will give you an effective means with which to pursue your self-interest. But of course the "invisible" hand (market forces) is causing you to promote the general interest at the same time by compelling you to provide quality shelter for people.

More Cash and Diversification with Every Step

This method permits step-by-step success that is confirmed by steadily increasing cash flow. Quitting is discouraged because success is realized every month. It is not like dealing in raw land, where you may not find out for sure if the deal is successful until you sell the land five to ten years later. You may end up getting trapped in the nasty position of being asset rich and income poor. With this condominium method, you insist on seeing real gains—on a regular basis—or you don't go on. You do not proceed with a purchase based on the speculation that price appreciation in the future will make up for today's real losses. This method enables you to understand and control the process to such a degree that you can have enough confidence to invest money you cannot afford to lose.

Also, this method allows the average condominium investor, who may not always select the very best condominium available, a low-risk way to succeed because it permits more diversification with every step. If you are not an expert stock picker, you should not concentrate your investment in one stock but rather diversify your investment by buying many different kinds. With condominiums you can easily diversify by location. Simply by buying into a number of different condominium projects, you will avoid the risk of concentrating all your real assets. It will thus take more than one mud slide to sweep them all away. You would not have this diversification by location if you owned just one apartment building.

BELIEVE IT OR NOT, YOU HAVE A TEAM

You can continue investing like this indefinitely; you shouldn't get tired of or worn out by it because if it is properly set up with carefully selected properties, most of the time you should be able to forget your condominiums and do other things. "Properly set up" means that in effect, you have a team of professionals taking care of all the routine but important details.

The team concept here is unlike one you might encounter in a large, complex, bureaucratic organization, where teams have time-consuming meetings and many times not much of a value-added nature gets accomplished. Your team will almost never have any meetings but will always know what to do for you to earn their premiums, commissions, or fees. The team will consist of your property manager, your banker, your real estate brokers (when you are buying and selling), the various condominium associations and managers, your tax accountant, and your insurance agent. They all should know their role automatically. Your team members are not your partners, and most of them can be relatively easily replaced if they are not performing their function more or less flawlessly. Neither are they employees on your payroll. You do not pay anyone for just showing up. You pay only for results.

Once you have your rental condominium team set up and running smoothly, you can take your hands off the handlebars and say, "Look, Ma, no hands." You wanted a money-making business without being involved in all the details on a regular basis? You got it. You have professionals organized to do everything for you except watch your money—and that job you should never give away to anyone else. You are responsible for the results of your investment. There should be very little stress and strain in watching the results—that is, keeping an eye on cash flow. This is an investment you can stay with a long time . . . forever, or indefinitely, whichever you prefer. Time is now your friend.

IN POSITION FOR WINDFALL PROFITS

The slowness of this method makes it virtually impossible for you to invest in a real estate bubble at the wrong time. However, if there is a real estate boom in your area, you will always be in a position to reap windfall profits. You won't be racing after the ball only to get there too late after the play is over. If real estate prices jump up sharply, you will see your get-rich-quick dreams start coming true, at least on paper. Or if your area is hit by rapidly escalating rents, you will be all set to realize excellent profits in the form of rapidly swelling cash flow. And, of course, because increases in rents are usually followed by (if not anticipated by) increases in the value of the underlying real estate, you will probably also experience paper gains sooner or later. Investment-grade condominiums enable you to have more than mere pipe dreams about winning the lottery or hitting the jackpot in a Reno casino.

FINAL INVESTMENT REQUIREMENT: EXISTENCE

Getting started will require some persistence in buying the right condominiums and then some patience to give the condominiums time to prove themselves, but after you have had them for a few years, you will know what to expect from them. The income you will derive from them will become so stable and reliable that you will take it for granted. You may have the feeling that the only thing required for this investment to continue to work for you is mere existence. This is just another way of saying that time is now a really good friend of yours.

Chapter 5

Why Condominiums and Not Apartments or Houses?

It Is So Easy: Buy a Good House That Just Needs a Little Paint

In the early 1970s, many books were written and many seminars were given on how to make money in real estate. There was a good reason for this: Inflation was driving real estate prices through the roof. I went to some of these seminars and read some of these books, but the methods presented required more time, work (including real, hands-on skilled labor), and expertise in real estate than I had to offer.

The Right-Things-Wrong Method Is Wrong for Beginners

Most of the books and seminars went into great detail on how to buy apartments or houses for a low price because they have the right things (cosmetic things that are supposedly easy to fix) wrong with them. Next, they tell you, you simply take care of these problems and rent out the restored property for a profit. After a short holding period, they usually suggest, you sell the property for a much higher price. But you don't stop here. You use the profits to do it again and again, bigger and better each time.

Sounds simple? I don't think so. If you don't agree, all you need to do is get one of these books and read it. As you are reading, visualize yourself actually doing all the things they tell you to do. I think you will see that a lot of work and devilish detail is involved in this method. You have to figure out what the *right* wrong things are and how much it will cost to fix them. You have to make sure there are no hidden *wrong* wrong things. You must then negotiate a low enough price to cover all your expenses for fixing up the place. You will also have to gain some skill in developing a method for selecting the right location. It is one thing to replace the wrong door with the right door and quite another thing to relocate from the wrong location to the right location. After you have acquired and restored the property to mint condition, all the details of managing and maintaining the whole place will be up to you. There will be no condominium association in place to take care of it.

If reading a book is not enough for you, go take a look at a run-down duplex. I did that once, and once was enough. As the real estate agent and I circled the building, all I saw was work, work, and more work. One drive around the building drove the idea of investment completely out of my mind. After looking at this fixer-upper duplex for five minutes, I asked the agent to drive me straight home to my new condominium!

THE SIMPLE CONDOMINIUM WAY

What I needed was the very simplest, least time-consuming way to invest directly in real estate. The reason, I suspect, I was not able to discover this method in a book or seminar was that it is so simple and obvious. There appears to be so little to it that no one probably thought it worthwhile to dedicate a whole book or seminar to it.

By chance I heard about some new, relatively inexpensive condominiums for sale. I took one or two looks and felt they would be easy to buy and rent. I bought one and rented it out for while. The experience confirmed my guess that this was the method for investing in real estate most suitable to me. I saw little risk and few unknowns. It stands to reason that because condominiums are much more carefree to own and live in than a house, that they would also be much easier to invest in.

THE EVERYTHING-RIGHT METHOD IS RIGHT

Without the help of a how-to book, after years of trial and error with many different kinds of investments, I had finally come across a form of investment that was right for me. Large numbers of other people are obviously also investing in this way; someone has to own all those rental condominium units out there. As of 1995 there were about 5.2 million condominium units in the United States, and I estimate that about 30%, or 1.6 million, are rental units owned by about eight hundred thousand condominium landlords.[1] I don't know what all those other owners of rental condominiums think about their investments, but I view my condominiums as a distinct method of investment that yields superior results. This method might be called the "buy a condominium unit that has everything right with it and rent it out forever" method—"forever," that is, as long as it makes money and gives you very little trouble. By *trouble,* I mean frequent demands upon your free time caused by your ownership of a given condominium. A high rate of vacancies or a lot of repairs could, for example, require you to have discussions with your property manager more often than you would prefer.

WITH LIMITED KNOWLEDGE, LIMIT WHAT YOU DO

This method allowed me to invest in real estate, early enough to make a difference, with limited knowledge about real estate. The method attacks the problem of never knowing enough about such a broad subject as real estate by limiting your activities to a very small area within that vast field of knowledge. You narrow your focus down to what you can actually see and really understand—one condominium unit. It is relatively easy to grasp what you are getting into because usually you will get exactly what you see. There will be much less chance to make an error in judgment due to a lack of skill, knowledge, or experience. By buying into only new or mint-condition condominium projects, you can avoid a host of problems that would be best tackled by someone else. For example, you should not have to assess the cost of deferred repairs and maintenance. And later, you should not be caught in a position of trying to catch up on these deferred repairs and maintenance because you made a mistake in the assessment. All this is not meant to imply that more knowledge is somehow bad; on the contrary, possessing more knowledge at the start should improve the quality of your investment decisions.

GET IN AFTER THE BIG RISKS HAVE BEEN TAKEN

In applying this method, you leave the significant risks involved in finding the right location and the construction of your future rental unit to the condominium project's developer. Two of my best condominium investments are in projects where the developers had a tough time completing and selling out the project fast enough to make a decent amount of money. And in one case I heard a rumor that the developer lost money. I had based my decision to buy on an early sales rate that was quite rapid: Less expensive units on lower floors were snapped up quickly, but sales slowed to a crawl later for the more expensive units, generally the ones higher up in the building.

Unfortunately, my views about the risks of developing real estate are not just based on reading, observation from afar, hearsay, and rumor. I also have gained personal experience on the matter. For $2,500 I became a limited partner in a partnership that was developing some nice, new condominiums for people to buy and live in. The condominium project was completed, and all the units were sold to new condominium homeowners. The project was successful from the new homeowners' point of view but was a failure from the point of view of those who put up the money to develop it. The total cost of developing the project was greater than the proceeds from sales. The limited partners' losses were indeed limited—limited to the full amount of their investment—no more, no less.

This was a $2,500 lesson that taught me that I did not know how to make money building condominiums, even with the help of general partners who were supposed to be experts.

SAFETY IN NUMBERS—CONDOMINIUM HOME BUYERS ARE NOT LEMMINGS

Fortunately, in looking for an investment-grade condominium unit to buy, you don't have to rely on just the developers' expert judgment as to the location and the ultimate value of the project. You can also rely on the collective judgment of many other people who make their demands known in the condominium market. You want to buy in with people who are seeking to find just the right condominium at the right price as their new home. That people are buying them as their new home is very important. They should not be purchasing the units merely because the prices are going up rapidly and hopefully will continue to go up. If there are too many speculators buying, you could encounter a dangerous, lemming-like situation. An overheated market occurs when price increases alone cause more people to pile on in a buying frenzy and thus generate still more price increases.

You should buy in only after you wait to see that a strong demand exists for units in the project for the right reasons. *Strong demand* means that a significant number of units are actually being sold every month. Only after the condominium in which you are interested has passed all these tests should you perform your own evaluation. You want to make sure that the place meets your standards (could you live there yourself?) and that you can clearly calculate a positive cash flow. These evaluations and calculations will tend to be very accurate because they will probably be based on rents actually collected from existing rental units in the condominium complex that are exactly the same or very similar. This procedure should lead you to desirable projects and prevent you from buying into a complex where the prices may have been driven too high by speculative fever. In this sense, condominiums provide safety in numbers.

If It Is Not a Condominium, It Is All Up to You

Contrast this with the analysis, evaluation, judgment, and calculation you would have to make in buying a duplex or a single-family home. You will have to rely much more on your own expertise in determining that the property has a good location and the price represents good value. I knew someone once who, using money borrowed from his mother, bought a fixer-upper house that was quite unusual in appearance. He viewed this unique appearance as a strength that would help it stand out in the market after he fixed it up. He planned to sell it quickly because his mother wanted to get back her life savings soon. Well, his taste in houses must have been too unusual, because there seemed to be no market for the house. It was agonizing to listen to him detail his desperate search for that rare buyer who might be out there with the same taste in houses. I heard that he finally did manage to sell the place for a substantial loss. When you deal in moderately priced condominiums, you are dealing in basic shelter for which a broad market can be sized up before you buy.

To be successful in applying the fixer-upper method, you should become a real estate expert to some degree before you start. Also, you should be ready to take on another job at least part time. Overall repairs and maintenance you will have to do yourself or make arrangements to have someone else do it. For example, you might have to plan to have the funds available for a new roof in five or ten years. And if you ever have bigger problems such as lawsuits, broken pipes, contractors failing to perform work as stated in the contract, or a major leak, you would have to take on those battles alone. In a condominium, the condominium association and the property management firm it hires are responsible for taking care of things like that. Duplexes and single-family homes don't come with built-in management. I was lucky enough to meet and informally interview a landlord with broader experience than I have had. This landlord has had experience renting out houses, apartments, and condominiums, and she maintains that houses and apartments are a lot more work.

INVESTMENTS YOU CAN REALLY WORK ON— IF YOU HAVE THE SKILL

If you read a comprehensive book on investing in fixer-upper single-family homes and small apartment buildings, you will get a much better idea about what is involved in that process. I cannot really discuss in any meaningful detail this method of investing in real estate because I never got beyond quickly reading some of those books, which seemed like they were trying to fix me up with another job. I was looking for profits, but found mostly instructions on how to do more work. Some of those books, in so many words, are telling someone with no experience in real estate to go right ahead, buy a fixer-upper, and basically fix it up by themselves. You are supposed to dig in and do some real hands-on work. On the job, you are expected to pick up some plumbing, carpentry, electrical, painting, and maybe some bricklaying skills, too. At the same time that you are becoming a jack-of-all-trades, you are supposed to find good tenants and keep them for a long time. This would be like a rock climber in a really tight spot trying to reposition all four limbs simultaneously instead of just one at a time as normally recommended. They say you learn from your mistakes, but you cannot afford too many mistakes on your very first investment. In the real world, just one major error can sometimes bring the learning opportunity to an abrupt halt.

However, to be optimistic, let us assume that you are a lucky, fast learner and that your learning on the job does not come at the price of too many costly mistakes. You work hard on a few more fixer-uppers successfully—your money is growing as well as your calluses. But are you ready to keep this up for 30 years? I know of some people with full-time careers who bought duplexes and small houses to rent out. They did it for a while and apparently were making money, but after a few years they sold out. They told me it was just too much work. Too many evenings and weekends had to be sacrificed. Another former landlord told me he made a lot of money from his real estate but sold everything because there were "too many headaches." And I read about an apartment owner who sold out after a tenant called him late at night to have a light bulb replaced. To be fair, I must add, I also know other people who have been renting out and managing their own apartments for a long time, and apparently they somehow accept the extra work they have given themselves. They seem ready to pull this extra burden for the long haul as an integral part of their lives. I even knew some people who lived in the fixer-upper house while they were renovating it. They sold the house as soon as it was in perfect condition and then moved into another run-down place they could work on again. They were making money, but most of the time they were living in a construction zone. This just goes to show you the many different ways (some more painful than others) to provide shelter to other people and, of course, make money in the process.

If you don't know what kind of landlord you are meant to be, you should find out before you actually invest your precious capital. You can find out by talking to landlords you know and by reading about it. If you know yourself, a book such as Leigh Robinson's *Landlording* should clearly tell you which way you should go in the business of providing shelter for other people. Robinson's book is a large detailed manual on how to be a landlord if you plan to do it all yourself. And right up front, in the preface to the seventh edition, revised, (1995), this expert landlord tells you like it is by closing with the following two sentences: "You will have to work hard and be vigilant on your own! Long may you prosper!" Robinson gives you an idea what this hard work is like: "These pages bear the marks of many interruptions to fix cold heaters, broken windows, outlets, wet-bottom water heaters, and so on and on. Sympathize, if you will, dear landlord or landlady. No one else will."[2] One of the main points of my book is that you may not be able to get anyone to sympathize with you, but you can pay someone to do the hard work and take care of all these ongoing issues. If you still cannot decide which way to go after looking at the size of this manual on landlording and reading the preface and introduction and looking at the table of contents, you should definitely attempt to read the whole book. That reading experience by itself may seem like hard work. Struggling through a book like that could be just as instructive as the lessons you might learn in the school of hard knocks (buying a run-down rental house or an apartment and just doing it), and you won't be putting any capital at risk.

You Can Work On It All—But Will It All Work Out for You?

According to some of these books' authors, a lot of people make money the fixer-upper way. However, some of the more conservative authors do warn the beginner that attaining a positive cash flow situation is not easy, at least for about the first three years. Peter Miller states that "around the country there are many investors who have accepted the reality of negative cash flow during the first several years of ownership in exchange for appreciation, tax benefits, and ultimately monthly income as well. Not a bad trade-off for those who can afford it."[3] And Milt Tanzer warns, "Any time you buy real estate that is 100 percent leveraged or financed, you can reasonably expect to have to 'feed' it to make it break even."[4] (This should not happen to you, if you follow the most conservative path I laid out in Chapter 3). This means that in a lot of cases, all that management and labor provided by the new fixer-upper landlord does not necessarily translate into better investment results than what a new condominium might provide without any supposedly free management and labor donated by the owner. Working long and hard like a dog might make some people feel good, but it is not a guarantee of success. One property might perform better than another property for a lot of different reasons, including factors such as cost, location, the quality of construction, and management. Location might be considered the most important factor in the overall scheme of things, but once you own a piece of property, the location is fixed; management then becomes the most important factor.

Good management will minimize your costs and maximize your revenues in any given residential property rental market. The owners of any rental unit should not give the management job to themselves unless they are without a doubt very good property managers; if not, they will know for sure that they are not paying a management fee to someone else, but they may never be sure how much more they are losing elsewhere. For example, I could take back the management of one of my weaker units and thus increase its cash flow by 9% by not having to pay the property management fee—if everything else stayed the same. I could also do the cleaning, painting, and repairs myself and maybe increase cash flow by another 2% to 3%—if everything else stayed the same. All this work, assuming I could do it successfully—keeping the vacancy rate, other costs, and rents the same—would increase my cash flow from this weaker unit to where it would be about equal to one of my best-performing units. But this application of so-called free labor does not transform this poor performer into a better investment in the long run. The fact that I, the owner, provided some hands-on labor and found my own tenants will not make the rental unit appreciate any more in value. Assuming I managed just as well as the property managers I replaced, I would have simply earned some extra cash for myself by giving myself an extra job.

But everything else will *not* stay the same for very long; something will inevitably change. The level of rents, the vacancy rate, or other costs could fluctuate. My cash flow expectations may or may not be met while I am on the job as manager and general caretaker. If expectations are not met and the cause is not entirely clear, doubts and questions of a personal nature could be raised in my mind. If I should wonder if the average vacancy rate is as low as possible, or if I should wonder whether the average rent represents good value given the vacancy rate, I would probably also wonder if I hired an adequate professional property manager when I hired myself. I might begin to wonder if I am paying my way even though I work for nothing. I might even stop wondering and replace myself with a professional to see if that makes a difference. What a great way to make a difference: Find someone else to do your work for you. You can now step back out of the view of the tenants and the repair and maintenance people and become for all practical purposes an *invisible* landlord. You will still be there nearby to guide things in your favor, but now you will operate in a more indirect manner, as does the invisible hand.

IF INVESTMENT CONDOMINIUMS DID NOT EXIST, COULD YOU CREATE ONE?

To more fully appreciate condominiums as an investment vehicle, consider what your options might be for investing in income-producing real estate if condominiums did not exist. You could attempt to simulate a condominium situation by finding a duplex or a small house in mint condition and learning how to contract out as much of the management and work as possible. I imagine that this, even on a small scale, could be done profitably. I have not tried it personally, but you can already see that it will be more of a hassle. You will either have to learn how to do more of the work yourself or how to contract for more efficient help at a reasonable cost.

However, let us say you could learn how to create a condominium-like structure by contracting out all the management;

do you go for a couple of rental single-family houses or a duplex? Do you invest in apartments, because they might be easier to manage, or would houses be the preferable vehicles for investment, because of potentially better resale value? For example, the first condominium I sold commanded a higher price than rental income alone would justify because it was sold as a condominium home and not just as income property (like an apartment). A rental single-family house could also possibly be sold as a home (not as rental property) and thus fetch a higher price if the yard and everything else has been maintained by you or your management to a homelike standard.

Perhaps the best alternative to a condominium could be an apartment with very strong homelike qualities (many apartments like that, in fact, are converted to condominiums). The value of your high-quality apartment would still normally be closely related to the net rental income that it can produce, but this relationship would now be more advantageous to you because places for rent that are more homey will tend to have lower vacancy rates and higher rents. But even a quality upscale apartment building that is large will not be able to offer one thing that many renters are seeking: a place where they can live and not be surrounded by a large number of other renters. They know that owners are generally more interested in keeping up a place than renters. A condominium building with a low percentage of rental units will provide them with the mixed social environment they need, and they will be ready to pay a higher rent to get into the few condominium units available for rent. So it is not just the superior location and amenities that can make a good condominium unit more profitable than an investment in apartments.

INDIRECT INVESTMENTS IN INCOME-PRODUCING REAL ESTATE

If you could not get a positive cash flow or it is too much work for you to invest directly into residential income-producing real estate of any kind but you still feel you need real estate in your investment portfolio, you can do it more indirectly. You could get into a limited partnership or go to the stock market and buy shares in a real estate investment trust (REIT). But as you are considering these more indirect investments, keep in mind that the money you invest will be coming directly out of your bank account and its loss would be felt directly by you.

SET YOUR LIMITED PARTNERSHIP LIMITS TO ZERO

I have participated in quite a few limited partnerships that invested mostly in apartments. The results have not been good. Some provided a good return, but too many others turned out to be a total loss. Depending upon how my few remaining ones perform, I don't know for sure whether I'll break even or have a small loss or gain from all of my limited partnerships. From my experience, I would not recommend them to anyone who is looking for a conservative, low-risk investment.

In general, I would say that most of the limited partnerships in which I invested were high risk because of the high fees paid to the managing partners, the large amount of leverage used, and the overly optimistic projections for rent increases and inflation on which the partnership was based. A combination of high fees and too much leverage can make a real estate investment as risky as speculating in commodity futures. Excessive management and debt expense can doom even a good piece of income property to failure as an investment. And many times the property selected is not that good. When selecting slightly distressed properties to buy for the partnership, all too often managing partners have been wrong about how right the wrong things were and the value of the price discount they were getting for the right wrong things. Owing to a combination of reasons like this, the return on investment from these slightly distressed properties was quite depressed relative to expectations. This deadly combination can kill you financially if you get too involved.

CAN YOU PICK THE RIGHT REIT?

I have never invested in a REIT (Real Estate Investment Trust), but because you are investing in the stock market when you buy shares of a REIT, being a good REIT stock picker would be essential, because in 1973 and 1974 many REITs plunged and lost as much as 80% to 90% of their value.[5] Some of these REITs, I am sure, owned fine buildings built to last—solid like the pyramids. But for the investor in these buildings who was not aware that the market for them had become too speculative, all that seemed solid melted into thin air.

With limited partnerships I proved to myself that just based on the numbers, I could not pick out only the good ones. But a REIT is normally more liquid. You could sell your shares much more easily if your REIT started taking a turn for the worse and thus minimize your losses or lock in your profit—*if* you acted fast enough. This is a really big if, because selling shares at the right time is a big psychological problem for many share owners. So many REIT investors could not make that telephone call to say "sell" fast enough in 1973 and 1974. And if they decided to sell a little too late, they probably were not able to sell easily, because when markets go down fast, they tend to go illiquid. They maximized their losses by failing to take action at the right time. REITs enable you to make a liquid investment in real estate but that liquidity, which can dry up in a blink of an eye, does not necessarily make them as safe as a few personally chosen and tested condominiums.

SOME CONDOMINIUM CONS

The main point of this book is that condominiums can be great vehicles for investing in real estate. But they are not perfect. Condominiums may have some disadvantages in certain situations. I have been pointing out drawbacks to some other ways of investing in real estate, so it is only fair to consider an aspect of investing in condominiums that you may encounter and perceive as negative. You may at times view the whole condominium structure and its ramifications as having flipped from the pro to the con column. For example, if the condominium association decides that a special assessment is needed, you will have to pay it regardless of whether you like the timing or agree with the amount or the reason for the assessment. And some condominiums are not insured against earthquakes because a majority of the owners have voted against the additional cost of an earthquake insurance premium. You may want earthquake insurance but may not be able to get it because most of the other owners don't want it. This is another thing to look into before you buy a particular condominium. By having the benefits of built-in management, you lose some flexibility and give up some control over your property.

The rules can vary from condominium to condominium; you should check them out carefully. Some rules might be quite restrictive and have a negative cost impact in the short run but may actually be to your advantage in the long run. For example, the board of trustees in one of my condominiums now has a move in/out fee of $200, and two interview sessions with the resident manager (one prior to moving in and the second shortly after moving in) are required for any prospective owner, renter, or lessee at a cost of $25 each for a total of $50. I do not consider this a negative development because I do not have a high tenant turnover rate in this condominium. And if a rule like this discourages the increase or reduces the number of rental units in the building, this might actually increase the value of my unit in the long run.

A single-family home rental, I have read, has an advantage in this regard because you do not have any condominium homeowners association dues or special assessments and the tenants take care of the lawn and the yard. For me to be convinced that this is any kind of a significant cost advantage, I would have to believe that single-family homeowners do not ultimately pay for most of the things that my condominium dues provide for. Also, I would have to believe the unbelievable: that tenants will take care of the lawn in the same way as the owners and professional gardeners at my various condominiums. If you are in the residential income property business for the long run, you will have to pay your dues in one form or another sooner or later. There is no such thing as a free lunch.

SKIP THE TENANTS, SKIP THE MANAGEMENT— THE RAW LAND METHOD

A way to invest in real estate with even less trouble than this income-producing condominium method might be to buy some raw land. Once you have it, all you have to do is simply wait for it to appreciate in value and then sell it for a profit. I have never tried this method because it does not meet my requirement for a steady cash flow to continually confirm that I am doing the right thing. There seems to be too much hope and not enough steady cash in raw land. But if you insist on relying on hope or just do not want to share your condominiums with tenants (keep them fresh until you sell them), this method can also be applied to condominiums. I once saw it applied to units like mine. An individual bought two condominium units, near one of my rental units, and just kept them vacant, apparently waiting to sell them later for a gain. In effect, he was treating them like an investment in raw land. But that means the gain from appreciation would have to make up for all the buying, financing (if any), and selling costs in addition to property taxes and condominium fees paid during the holding period. Also, homes unoccupied for an extended period of time will tend to deteriorate faster than a home that has been carefully occupied. This deterioration from mildew, rust, and must, if allowed to go on for too long, could reduce the resale price. Granted, this was a period of high inflation, but unless his timing of the sale was perfect, I doubt that there would have been a big gain if and when he sold them. Inflation did not continue at the high rate we had gotten used to and come to expect. Empty condominiums, however, are not really raw land. If he still has them, he has something of economic value that he can rent or sell; this is not always true for real raw land.

I was acquainted with speculators who bought desert land near Los Angeles in anticipation of a new airport being built out there in the 1960s. They gained a real-life experience from real raw land. The airport was not built, and the tracts of desert—that real estate brokers had bundled up for them to buy in nice, neat $10,000 packages—now basically have no economic value. There was no magic bullet to be found in all that empty space to save them. Jackrabbits do not have the necessary dollars to make their demands known in the real estate marketplace.

How about Industrial and Distressed Property?

I learned enough about investing in industrial and distressed property to realize that it was out of my area of expertise. Luckily, the lesson on industrial property was free, but the lesson on investing in distressed property was unforgettable because its price was $2,500.

I once considered investing in an industrial property development project. After listening to a presentation on the project, I understood enough to realize that it was a long, complicated affair. It was so full of unknowns that the developer could not predict when there might be any kind of a return on my investment. However, the developer could go on at length discussing the concept, and he was eager to take my money and apply it to fleshing out his ideas with more specific plans. Betting on this concept would have really been a long shot. I left the presentation, having gotten a free introduction to the world of developing industrial parks.

Now, you might think that buying distressed property for a price below market value and soon thereafter selling it for a much higher price would be a sure thing. How can you miss on a deal like that? Buy low, sell high—the age-old way to make money. But how do you actually do this? I knew enough to know that I did not know how to do it, so for $2,500, I bought into a limited partnership that claimed to know how to do it. The supposedly expert general partners had worked out detailed procedures on how to pick up real estate that is about to go into default at bargain-basement prices. Their procedures seemed well thought out. They had a step-by-step plan. They knew where and when to go to court for a specific piece of distressed property that was being disposed of. They would even know in advance just the right time and from which pocket they were going to pull out the required cash to take possession of the property. The general partners' attention to detail seemed impressive.

I don't know why they failed to make money. I was not involved in the process; I just gave them my money. Maybe they could not buy low enough. Maybe they could not sell high enough. Maybe it was a combination of both. Maybe they were hoping for more inflation to come to the rescue.

For me, this was a $2,500 lesson—real estate investment can be tricky and full of pitfalls if you stray out of your area of proven competence.

You can also try to make money in real estate by developing lots for residential homes. I know someone who has done this successfully, and he has described it as a frustrating bureaucratic struggle, so I have not bothered to get a more direct lesson in this aspect of real estate investment.

YOU REALLY JUST DON'T KNOW WHAT IS AHEAD OF YOU

Some observers claim that condominiums do not increase in value as fast as single-family homes. Condominiums can be constructed to permit greater density, and that greater density makes condominiums subject to more overbuilding. This would explain, they say, why more condominiums than houses are being built in some areas, in spite of condominiums being less popular than houses. (In King County, Washington, net sales of new condominiums outpaced sales of new single-family homes during the first three quarters of 1996.)[6] On a total statistical basis, however, creeping condominiumism is not about to dominate the housing market anytime soon because of the roughly one hundred million housing units in the country, only about 5% are condominiums.[7] Most people, they say, still prefer a house they can completely walk around. They want a home sitting on a piece of land they can call their own. (How sad that in a condominium you can never say, "This land is all mine." You have to say something like, "Three percent of this land is all mine.") But not everyone who prefers a house ends up in a house. They may start out looking for a house, but owing to cost and other considerations, such as quality, they end up in a condominium. A buyer of a $124,000 condominium who at first had looked at houses put it more bluntly: "I looked at homes in the hundred-thirties that were absolute junk."[8] The powerful forces of supply and demand will not allow the condominium and house markets to run away from each other. The cost link can be stretched a bit but not broken. As a result, what "they" say about condominiums is not always true everywhere. The condominiums I have in the more densely populated areas have appreciated the most. And greater density is still being created there due to the construction of even more new apartments and condominiums. The amount of this appreciation was also greater than what some single-family homes experienced nearby.

I know that all of my condominiums appreciated much more than an average single-family home in Los Angeles, where it is estimated that single-family homes decreased in value by about 16% in recent years (1995 to 1996). The point here is that real estate markets are very local, and generalized statements about their value on a national basis could be very misleading. For example, would the following general national statistics help you make a better investment decision in your particular local market? Would it help you to know that June Flecher stated in the August 30, 1996, *Wall Street Journal* that "from 1993 to 1995 condominiums appreciated 5.03% a year according to the National Association of Realtors, while single-family homes rose 5.71% annually"?[9] Based on these statistics, we now know that single-family homes across the country did appreciate on average a little bit more than condominiums in those two particular years. Does this mean you can make more money investing in single-family homes in your locality?

But on the other hand, other statistics indicate that a single-family home may not be such a good deal. The Dow Jones Real Estate Index shows that from 1990 to 1996, luxury homes in 25 metro areas in the United States increased in price by only 23.44%, or about 3.91% a year.[10] Which rate of appreciation do you think will apply to the real estate you are going to buy? You can make your best guess, but, of course, you don't know. Only if you are unwise will you foolishly think that you do.

So where does all this lead us? If you believe that the national statistics of your choice will tell you what is ahead of you, it could lead you to take any number of dangerous forks in the road. You could switch to buying single-family homes that you may not be able to properly manage. On the other hand, believing in another set of statistics, you could start to speculate in condominiums.

For example, if you believed that every year you could count on that 5.03% appreciation for condominiums, you could then use leverage (borrowed money) without any worry and make a lot of easy money. You could buy a $100,000 condominium by making a $5,000 down payment and borrowing the rest. Now, let us say you rent it out and you have a break-even situation; your costs are covered by the rent, but nothing more is left over. In a situation like this, you are not getting any cash out of your condominium, but if it really goes up in price, say, by 5% (0.03% less than expected) on paper, you would be making a 100% return on your investment of $5,000 in the first year. A 5% price increase for a $100,000 condominium is $5,000, and that is equal to 100% of your down payment. In the second year, it would be a 105% gain on paper ($105,000 times 5% divided by $5,000 and then multiplied by 100%). With gains like this, shouldn't you borrow as much as you can (as much as the money lenders are permitted to loan to you) and have as many condominiums like that as possible? Before you do anything like that, I should point out that the Dow Jones Real Estate Index for Luxury Homes went down in three metro areas from 1990 to 1996: Los Angeles, San Diego, and Washington, D.C. decreased by 17%, 10%, and 3%, respectively. Is your metro area forever immune from a downward trend in any sector of real estate, including less expensive condominiums? For King County, Washington, as Appendix H shows, homes increased in price by an average (based on seven years) of 6.2%, but that 6.2% average includes a 26.4% price increase for 1990 and a 0.4% decrease for 1991—so how can anyone know what, exactly, lies ahead next year?

If you are wise, you will know that you really do not know what lies ahead; thus, in each new condominium you acquire, you should insist on seeking instant gratification in the form of monthly cash flow. This practice will keep you from taking a dangerous, speculative fork in the road.

Chapter 6

Condominiums versus Stocks and Bonds

WHAT DO YOU WANT TO WORRY ABOUT, A STOCK MARKET CRASH OR EARTHQUAKES?

Over the past 18 years, my condominiums have given me a gain averaging about 20.8% a year.[1] Some of the mutual funds I own increased in price by 30% in 1995. So I look at my investment portfolio and ask myself, Why do I still have such a large part of my assets invested in condominiums and such a small part in stocks when the stock market is having some of the best gains in a long time? The main reason, I think, is that the stock market (Dow Jones industrial average) dropped like a rock (that is, by 45%) not so long ago—from 1,052 points in 1973 to 578 points in 1974. Worse still, some studies reported in the *Wall Street Journal* have concluded that the stock market may be overvalued by 60%. That was my evaluation of the stock market in 1998. Now in 2001, the NASDAQ has lost about 60% of its value. The Dow also continues to go down and the possibility of recession is looming.

Is there another sickening plunge in store for us? Well, I don't know, but my impression is that although a lot of economists argue about whether a Great Depression could occur again, there does not seem to be too much argument about the possibility of something like the 1974 adjustment reoccurring. In the year 2001, as more and more companies report lower and lower earnings and the economy continues to weaken, the possibility of another 1974 increases. And that would kill a lot of people financially. Professional investment advisors who are well aware of the past will tell you not to get emotional about your investments, but if you are heavily invested in the stock market and you are faced with possibilities like that, how can you *not* get emotional? Peter Lynch (one of the most successful mutual fund managers ever) has said that besides good research, you mainly need a strong stomach to invest in stocks. The stock market can wreak havoc on your mind, stomach, and wallet. When it starts plummeting like an airliner that hits clear-air turbulence, you don't know where and when it will stop. I have a difficult time imagining my condominiums doing something like this to me; I am not aware of any nervous fluctuations in some national condominium price index that is reported in the news every day. A boring condominium rental unit might even be quite suitable to some investors with a weak stomach.

As recently as 1987 there was a significant one-day drop in the Dow (about 20%) to remind us that stocks can be quite volatile. However, this was not a serious reminder but just a big, fast correction caused by programmed trading and panic. It turned out not to be a really catastrophic decline. The carnage was limited, unlike the really gloomy extended crashes I remember in 1968 and 1974, when the bad news went on and on for so long that most people seemed to be affected and disturbed by it. That would have been the right time to put into action that great idea: Buy really low, when everyone else is depressed. But it is difficult to buy if you are in a dark cloud yourself and everything around you looks like a bottomless pit. There seemed to be no bottom to the market; it was in a free fall. There had been warnings for 18 months, but few got out in time. People all around were losing a lot of money, and despair affects one's judgment. It was too much of a shock after the go-go era for stocks in the 1960s. The stock market had not just hit a small air pocket; the bubble had burst, and wealth was disappearing into thin air. And now again in 2001 significant amounts of wealth are disappearing into thin air as the dot-com companies continue to fall like inverted pyramids. The Dow lost 300 points in one day in early August 1998. But at the same time the climb of home prices topped inflation.

Now, the stock market has a lot of novice investors in it who have never experienced any really long-lasting downturn and do not fully appreciate the risks of stock trading. The dot-com disaster in 2001 is, relatively speaking, just a small taste of how bad it can get. The lack of this kind of experience will enable the stock market to climb to even riskier heights. But what will happen if another adjustment to the stock market occurs, one about as large as 1987's except that it does not bounce back for years? What will all these novice investors do? The booming stock market has, in effect, been training them to make a big mistake. Experts on stock market psychology are not sure about the answer to this question; every day on television you can watch them debate questions like this without conclusive results.

I never get to listen to any good debates about the psychology of the market for rental condominiums. Markets that are relatively stable and predictable do not provide much opportunity for such discussions. In contrast to what happened on Wall Street, the gross rents from my condominiums in 1987 increased by 14%. I would be hard pressed indeed to identify the psychological factors behind this real gain. It just happened. The negative financial environment in 1987 did not prevent my condominiums from performing well in the real economy on Main Street. My condominiums are very insensitive to the stock market; in fact, they seem to ignore Wall Street and all the worries about Asian markets in 1998 and everything else that went along with it. The waves created by the financial typhoons hitting Asia may sooner or later slam into and wipe out some real estate tycoons in this country who are exposed to a large amount of debt. Debt-free condominiums like mine may at most experience a small ripple effect from this global financial crisis. I am fully prepared to see my condominiums bob up and down a bit like corks in a pond disturbed by a few ripples.

From personal experience I can tell you that volatility in the stock market continues to keep investors jumping to the present day. The price of a technology mutual fund in which I have invested (using only a small amount of speculative cash) has gone up 20% and then down 40% in a very short period of time. The only thing I can think of that would so suddenly and adversely impact all of my condominiums, because they are geographically dispersed, is a big earthquake. They say that the Seattle area has a 10% chance of experiencing a really big one in the next 50 years. And if the earthquake were big enough, it could generate new facts on the ground that would render false all those statements about how safe it is to invest in a condominium. So is it better to tie your good fortune to the Richter scale or the Dow Jones index? Upon reflection, I always feel that when the only thing I can come up with to worry about is an earthquake, my investments must be in pretty good shape. And besides, condominiums can sometimes (see "Some Condominium Cons" in Chapter 5) be insured against earthquakes, but I have not heard of an active market for insurance against stock market crashes. Who could afford the insurance premium?

However, many experts say that over a 30-year period, a well-diversified portfolio in the stock market, held continuously, can be expected to return about 10%. That includes dividends and all the sharp peaks and valleys in the price of your stocks. You do have a choice. Do you want to move on up to affluence by taking the escalator or a roller coaster? This is not to say that real estate is not subject to market cycles, but in a well-diversified economic area, this is usually felt as a slow yin-and-yang process that is quite soothing compared to the yo-yo-like stock market. When things get bad and people lose confidence, they can dump their financial assets, but even in times of panic, they still need a roof over their heads. In a given year, income-producing real estate may not beat the stock market, but a few good condominiums in your portfolio will help alleviate some of the fear of being in the stock market year in and year out.

STABLE, PREDICTABLE CASH FLOW

In contrast to so many of my stocks, my condominiums are stable, relatively predictable, and provide a return that is superior to what the average investor can expect from the stock market over the long run. The cash flow I have received from rents in the last few years has been especially worry free, almost like getting an interest payment from a bond (I am not saying that rental income from condominiums is as guaranteed as interest payments are from bonds). In this regard, you could say my condominiums are now boring. Rents are increasing steadily, and their average price is appreciating quite a bit faster than inflation. I was writing this in about 1997, but in 1998 and 1999 price appreciation increased to as much as 15% a year, and only slowed down a bit in 2000 and 2001. I looked at some old records from 1982 and saw that my condominiums were, at one time, more exciting than the increases in 1998 and 1999 and than the stock market before the recent collapse.

PROTECTION FROM INFLATION

The 1970s were an era of accelerating inflation; some people thought they would never again see single-digit inflation and interest rates and that hard assets such as gold and real estate were going to make almost everyone rich (mutual funds seem to have taken over this role in 1995). This acceleration continued to impact my condominiums into 1982; by then, the rate of return on my investment was about 64% (at this point I had put in about 25% of my own money and had borrowed the rest). A great return on investments like this, of course, includes every type of a gain I could estimate at that time. Back then, I estimated, I was gaining 46% from appreciation (see what high leverage and inflation, in combination, can do), 9% from tax savings, 5% from cash flow, and 4% from equity buildup (due to amortization). Rates of return of this magnitude continued for a number of years.

Will we ever see a boom like that again? It is possible, of course; high home prices were making front-page headlines in Seattle newspapers in late 1997 once again, but I'm not counting on anything of that magnitude occurring anywhere in the near future.[2] I'll be satisfied if my condominiums continue to plod on about the same as they are doing right now. If my condominiums get exciting again, it will also probably mean that double-digit inflation has returned, and as a result a big piece of the exciting gains won't be real. Also, the smaller part of my portfolio that is in stocks and bonds would probably suffer terribly.

SUPERIOR NET PROFIT MARGIN

The end of a real estate boom may have significantly reduced the exciting paper gains from price appreciation, but my condominiums continue to yield—in a more normal real estate market—superior net profit margins. The net profit margin, or net income, as percent of sales (rents) for my condominiums is about 50% (excluding depreciation). For stock companies, a net margin above 15% for 12 months would be an indicator to some expert analysts that a company has a unique advantage in the marketplace.

LESS ANALYSIS, MORE REAL GAIN

Stocks and bonds are a much smaller percentage of my portfolio than are my condominiums. But for some reason, much more of my time is spent on watching and analyzing stocks than on the real stars in my portfolio, my five remaining condominiums. The news media is full of stock market news daily. Individual stocks are rated by experts. Worries are expressed continually about the market being too high (of course, there always are some expert voices raised saying the market could go still higher). More and more analysts expect a stock market drop of some kind; it could be a plunge or just a long, soft landing. Which do you prefer? Here again, this was my view of the stock market in about 1997, but now, reporting in 2001, we have experienced plunges and significant downward fluctuations and are now supposedly "searching for the bottom."

As recently as July 6, 2001, there was a 227-point drop (2.2%) to 10,253 in the Dow and a 76-point loss (3.6%) in the NASDAQ, down to 2,004. The turbulence in the stock market continues.

Listening to all this, we are continuously reminded that unless we actually manage to buy low and sell high, the gains we have made in the stock market are only paper gains. We cannot help but realize that all our unrealized gains may very well not be ours to keep for very long. They could all be pulled away from us by a downturn in the stock market. And if we are automatically reinvesting our stock dividends (real gains), all our gains in the stock market are relentlessly subject to stock market risk. We will have realized nothing. The reinvested dividends, along with paper gains, could be easily converted to one big paper loss by market action. Markets don't care; they treat old value and new value equally. Markets will just as easily wipe out old paper gains as value gained from recent stock purchases. If we should then sell in dismay, we would realize this paper loss. The stock market does not have a safety net.

More and more sophisticated analysis is different from making more and more money. If you want to do a lot of analysis, you will be out of luck with your rental condominiums; once they are set up and running smoothly and you are not planning to expand by buying another, there is not much for you to do but watch the cash flow. More analysis won't increase that. And even though you may get the cash flow in the form of a paper check, it is, of course, not merely a paper gain. It is real (your checks should never bounce around like the stock market). A few, quick, negative fluctuations in some market can no longer rob you of your gain.

You are also less likely to kid yourself if you focus on cash flow and pay less attention to rosy projections. You will know when you have to really jump in and take action. If the cash does not flow as normal, it will get your attention, and you will be compelled to do something about it. A direct hit in your pocketbook is an effective wake-up call. If rental income starts declining, you know you have a real problem. Real hard analysis then would be needed to make sure you do the right thing to fix it.

But let us say you experience a positive cash flow, as I have, over a long period of time; you will encounter the problem of trying to get a good return on that cash accumulating in your bank account or money market. This is the downside of realizing gains on a regular basis. Condominiums do not come with an automatic reinvestment plan. When you stop expanding, you are much safer from the danger of being overextended, but the accumulated cash flow from rental income is not safe from inflation and low interest rates in money markets.

NOT EXPANDING HAS ITS RISKS, TOO— REAL GAINS CONVERTED TO PAPER LOSSES

Unless you buy another condominium, you will have to do something else with this cash coming in from your condominiums. You can spend it all, which is not wise because you should always have a reserve to cover unexpected problems. You can leave the cash in a money market and try to not worry about it. But if you do that, you may barely be keeping up with inflation in the long run. I once had a professional financial planner review my portfolio; he said I had far too much cash on hand in the money market than could be justified by any possible contingencies I might face with my condominiums. And, of course, his solution to my hoarding problem was for me to buy some mutual funds he had for sale. Great! Is inflation risk worse than the risk you face with some mutual funds you don't understand?

As we discussed in Chapter 3, you can put some money back into the condominiums you have by paying off the mortgages. But there is a limit to that, and after you have paid off the mortgages, the cash builds up even faster. So inevitably, I think you will end up looking for another place to put at least some of this cash—a place where it can get a return that at least beats inflation and taxes. Another place for your cash won't be hard to find. Every day the news media write and talk about another place to put your money. You cannot get away from it. We have come full circle back to where we started this chapter—the stock market. Stocks are easy to buy into, but are they safe—like your condominiums on Main Street?

It would be tragic to take the real cash gains from your condominiums and convert them to paper losses in the stock market. This can be done all too easily by buying some stocks or stock mutual funds at the wrong time. You cannot tell in advance that it is the wrong time; you find out only after it is too late. You know it was the wrong time after the price of the stocks you purchased has gone down by about 10%. Then all you can do is watch them go down, down, down and then wait forever for them to come back up. If you have not yet had the experience, you will find that it is not easy to minimize your losses by simply selling everything quickly. Many veteran investors in stocks say that deciding when to sell a stock is more difficult to do (regardless of whether it is going up or down) than deciding to buy a stock.

In the 1960s there were numerous stories about people who had bought shares of Winnebago stock at a very low price and became millionaires on paper when Winnebago stock zoomed through the stratosphere. But a lot of these people managed to sell only after the value of their shares dove back down to the original purchase price. They rode their Winnebago shares up and then down again.

If your lack of previous experience with the stock market causes your wealth to dwindle, you might be very sorry that you did not stick with something you understand. You may wish you had taken the trouble to just buy another condominium, even if it was perhaps slightly overpriced. At least you would know that as long as there was some positive cash flow, you would hardly ever face the difficult decision to sell an income-producing condominium because the plan is to keep it indefinitely.

Whether you have had a sorry experience with other kinds of investments or not, sooner or later you should balance your portfolio. Even if you could find an unlimited supply of good investment-grade condominiums, a very large portfolio (relative to your total income from all sources) of 100% condominiums would be too illiquid. To balance your portfolio, you need to put something else in it that is more liquid, even though it may not be as safe and reliable as a condominium. The need for something else, like it or not, tends to lead us back to stocks and bonds.

It is said that stocks are meant for people whose main desire is to make money and bonds are meant for people who primarily fear losing any money. An investment-grade condominium can satisfy the desire for making money as well as alleviate the fear of losing it. But you can never get away from the fact that a condominium is real estate and can never be that something else. A pure condominium portfolio under certain economic conditions could lose its shine, just as gold did in the late 1990s, if it is not properly balanced with a good counterweight.

IT TAKES MONEY TO MAKE MONEY

I have been a small investor in stocks (small in terms of total dollars and of percentage of assets devoted to the stock market) for about thirty years. I have tried many different methods of investing and found that most of them work—some of the time.

Numerous times, I have been able to buy some stock for about four or five thousand dollars and then sell those shares for about a 40% gain six to eight months later. The percentage gains are great. It is a small thrill to actually succeed at buying low and selling high in specific instances. But you should not be surprised if I tell you that I cannot do this consistently. There are times when the stock goes down by about 30% to 40% after I buy it. I failed to heed Will Rogers's advice not to buy those stocks that go down. Most stock experts say that you should prevent this from happening to you by selling the stock as soon as it goes down by about 10%. I have managed to do that occasionally, but usually I hang onto them for three or four years through a business cycle until the stock price recovers to where I can sell it for a gain. Of course, I do have a few stocks that I have been holding for much longer than four years. I am still waiting for some of them to recover.

On the whole, I have done well (so far) in the stock market on a percentage basis, but the amount of dollars earned was usually not that significant. I could never really trust the stock market with any amount of cash that was meaningful (say, a year's salary) to me. I could play in the stock market only with money I felt I could afford to lose. A very long time, indeed, would be required to get affluent using this method with such a small amount of capital invested at any one time. To get rich quick in the stock market I would have to fairly consistently select stocks that go up by 300% to 400% at a rapid pace. Without the use of hindsight, I have found that I don't know how to do that.

Second Choice, Utilities

I had to find an investment into which I would dare invest for the long run as much as I would in another condominium but that would provide a better return than the money market or U.S. government bonds. Looking for such an investment, I read Benjamin Graham's bible on finance, *Security Analysis,* in which he clearly states that "the higher the degree of assurance that a given income will continue to be received, the higher the capitalized value of the income. As compared with both industrials and railroads, the electric utilities have a record of enviable stability."[3] I decided that electric utilities would be the best alternative to another condominium. They apparently have an enviable record similar to my condominiums. Utilities are considered by some financial advisors to be surrogate bonds, and because bonds are meant for people who don't want to take on any risk of losing their money, I thought that utilities would be my next most comfortable investment after condominiums. I bought a utility stock mutual fund, and it has more than doubled in value in eight years, mainly due to gains from the automatic reinvestment of dividends.

The amount I had the courage to put into this utility fund was $26,000. Eight years later, it was worth about $54,000. If I had used this $26,000 instead to buy two more condominiums for $130,000 (I would have had to borrow $104,000 to do this) and they increased in price at only 3% a year for the eight years, I would have gained more than $31,200 from appreciation alone, in comparison to the $28,000 gain in the utility fund. But buying another condominium does not diversify and balance the portfolio.

UTILITIES ARE EASIER

Utilities are better in one regard: They are even less trouble than my leisurely don't-get-your-hands-dirty-and-don't-ever-meet-the-tenants approach to investing in condominiums. Shares in utilities are much less difficult to buy, and you don't have direct responsibility for them. I intend to stick with them because of my experience with them so far and Benjamin Graham's analysis, which tells us that over a very long period of time, utilities have provided a fairly decent return. Also, utilities have held up well in bad times on Wall Street (but, of course, we cannot be sure how the restructuring of the marketplace for energy and the risks of nuclear power will affect this record in the future).

Because I really don't understand utilities, I decided to go for even more safety by buying a utility mutual fund. With a mutual fund, as the ads always claim, you get professional management and diversification. Both are important because diversification could save you when professional management fails you. I have diversified my condominiums by location, so diversification is certainly appropriate for investments in utilities. No matter how solid the investment appears, some diversification is important. Back in 1983, I remember watching a sad news report on television about a lady in her eighties who had invested her life savings (about $90,000) into Washington Public Power Supply System (WPPSS) municipal bonds and how she had lost all of it when these bonds went into default. And bonds are supposed to be safer than stocks! She had not diversified into anything else and had relied on assurances from bond salespeople that these bonds were absolutely safe. But when a reporter interviewed one of these WPPSS salespeople and asked him where he was investing his own money, he said, "Real estate."

To be safer still, I realized that I should not be diversified just among utilities but should get into other conservative mutual funds that invest in other kinds of stocks and bonds. A mutual fund that contains shares of numerous different kinds of large corporations would be even more difficult to really understand in depth, as you can a few condominiums. All you really have to go on is the mutual fund's past performance. As a result, your investment is usually based on faith and hope that the past performance of the mutual fund and its managers will continue to be about the same, or better, in the future. If you want a long, happy future, you should normally try to base it on a long, happy past.

As much as possible, base your faith and hope on a very long period of past performance; this will increase the chances of your faith being justified. The probability of what you hoped for coming true will be greater. If, for example, you take only 10 years as the period of past performance that you are going to use to guess about the future, you could be misled. There is a very good chance that a mere 10 years may have been exceptionally good ones. For example, you might read that "over the past 10 years, diversified U.S. stock funds gained an average 12.1% a year, compared with 13.8% for Standard & Poor's 500-stock index, according to fund Lipper Analytical Services."[4] From this statement, you might safely conclude that professional management was outperformed by the stock market as a whole for 10 years, but it could be dangerous to expect the stock market to gain an average of 13.8% a year for the next 10 years. In the year 2000, the S&P 500 Index went down by 9.10%, and, in early 2001, it continued on a downward trend.

In February 1997, Standard & Poor's 500-stock index had a price earnings ratio of 20 (normal is 13), yet people are putting money into the stock market as if they had never heard about buying low and selling high. It could be that the stock market has been going up for so long that some people have come to believe that it will continue to go up like that indefinitely. But isn't that like believing that the yang in yin and yang will never yang again? Now in 2001 the stock markets have taken a significant turn for the worse. Now hopefully many have come to finally realize that even in the "new economy," stock markets do not go up or down indefinitely.

UNDERSTAND, THEN INVEST

Many professional investment advisors will strongly advise you to invest only in things you understand. If you heed this warning, does that mean that all the assets you don't have in condominiums should be in a money market mutual fund or in a bank account? I sometimes wonder about this, as I watch even an index for utilities (my next best alternative to condominiums) fluctuate by as much as 40% over the years. Utilities are supposed to be an investment that is suitable for widows and orphans, but I don't feel that my surplus condominium money is as safe invested in utilities as it was when it was still tied up in condominiums. But what other choice is there besides the money market, a bank account, bonds, or utilities?

A government bond may feel safer than utilities in the short run, but over a longer period of time it may turn out to be a less safe place for the liquid part of your condominium investment owing to the effects of inflation upon a relatively low yielding investment such as a government bond.

There seems to be no way around it: To keep your condominium portfolio well balanced and liquid, you have to go on faith a little more and invest in things that can't be understood as well as a condominium. It is much easier to get the facts and understand in depth your investment in a few income-producing condominiums than to grasp your investment in just one multinational corporation. That is why a lot of people who invest directly in stocks of individual companies base their investment decisions on recommendations from someone else. Instead of doing a lot of basic research themselves about some very big company with global operations, many investors take a shortcut. They buy and sell stocks based on what a professional advisory service like Value Line, for example, thinks about that company.

The use of professional advice does not, of course, guarantee a better investment result because that advice is not infallible. You can see the proof of this by watching business programs on television. One professional analyst refused to do his job and make a buy or sell recommendation for a very large and complex corporation because "it has too many moving parts." Also, it was reported that another professional analyst, whose main task was to evaluate Motorola, recommended a buy for Motorola and then Motorola's stock proceeded to go down. The big problem for these professional analysts is that like anyone else, they do not know what will happen in the future, but they may also be frequently hampered in their responsibility of making predictions about the future by not having all the important information and data. I can use two local Pacific Northwest companies as an example of this lack-of-data problem. Boeing was being sued by stockholders in 1997 for not fully disclosing the extent of its schedule problems. Also many years ago, Olympia Beer Company did not disclose the fact that it had purchased millions of dollars of Penn Central securities that had plunged in value. You won't have such problems with your condominiums. They have very few important moving parts, mainly doors and windows. If you have your eyes wide open, you will usually get what you see. And if you make an unwise purchase with your condominium money, that is not a full-disclosure problem but a personal problem (unless you enjoy hiding things from yourself).

Value Line does not publish an opinion about your condominium. You have to get your own facts, and you have to do your own thinking. Luckily, hard thinking is not required all the time if you follow the path laid out in this book. You have to do some analysis only when you buy the condominium, and some more thinking might be required if it does not perform as normally expected. You have to think for yourself but not frequently.

YOU ARE AN INSIDER

You will tend to have a superior understanding of your investment in your condominiums not only because the investment is so simple and small, compared with investing in a large corporation, but also because you will be compelled to start thinking and acting like an insider who is directly involved in the operations of a business. You are not just going to be a passive shareholder somewhere far away, removed from what's going on. You won't be making critical decisions about what happens to your money based on recommendations from Value Line or anyone else. When you buy an income-producing condominium, you are not just buying a tiny share in some gigantic corporation. You are doing quite the opposite; you are buying the whole company and are going to be responsible for all of it. This profound realization will give you plenty of incentive to come to know your condominium inside out and to do your own independent thinking about it. Benjamin Graham says that this is the way you should act when you make any investments in the stock market: You should select any shares that you buy in a company with the same understanding and care you would exercise if you were, in fact, buying the whole company. When buying a condominium, you don't have to try to remember to do any acting. You will always be keenly aware that the condominium is 100% yours.

GET CLOSE TO YOUR INVESTMENT: LIVE IN IT!

You oversee the management of your condominiums by tracking cash flow and examining the monthly income statement. And if you have followed the most conservative path all along, you will also have lived inside your investment to really check it out, up close and personal. How's that for intimate knowledge of your investment? How many professional Value Line stock analysts have lived inside the company about which they are experts? But would you get a special insight into value of the stock by spending a night or two in a Coca-Cola bottling plant?

Additional inside information is gained on your investment by attending some of the condominium association meetings. At these meetings, the budget, maintenance, expenses, potential increases in condominium dues, and any special problems such as leaks that might require a special assessment to repair are discussed. You might want to attend a meeting like this at a condominium that may not be performing as well as the others or as normally expected from past experience. But usually you will find it is more efficient to keep up with what is going on with your investments by quickly reading the minutes of these meetings when they are sent to you.

UNDERSTANDING IS NOT A GUARANTEE

Understanding your investments, however, is not an end in itself. If a better understanding is not leading to a better return, then from a pure investment point of view, gaining this knowledge and understanding was a waste of time. If you could, over the long run, get a better return from an investment you don't understand as well, you would probably sacrifice understanding for higher profits. That is assuming you understand it well enough to know that the investment is not too super risky. You should probably know enough not to be in an investment where you can lose most of your money in a few days of dynamic market activity. If you have at least some level of understanding, then you are not betting everything on faith and luck.

If you are in an investment that you understand well enough to know that it is risky but think the return is worth the apparent risk, you should then know how to act quickly to minimize your losses if there is a market meltdown. And if you fail to act quickly enough, then you will simply have to understand that only time will tell if the investment will recover from its losses. For example, if for the last 20 years you had been lucky enough to have invested everything into Warren Buffet's Berkshire Hathaway company based on faith or belief in Warren Buffet, then you probably would not care that you violated Warren Buffet's own rule of not investing in anything he does not understand. His company has had a return over a very long time period that averages out (the returns fluctuate a lot from year to year) to more than 23% a year.

THE BEST INVESTMENT AT ANY PRICE?

So should we sell the condominiums that are returning less than 10% and buy shares in Berkshire Hathaway for about $54,000 a share (as of 1998)? I would say yes, if you are ready to bet that such performance for Hathaway will continue. I would not bet on that, however, because Hathaway's big investments in such companies as Coca-Cola and Gillette are not immune from the stock market and what happened to it in 1974 and 1987. If a 1974 situation did occur again and the stock market went down close to book value, only then might I think about selling a few condominiums and putting some of the proceeds in an investment like Berkshire Hathaway.

But even with the stock market at book value, liquidating any good real estate and putting it into Wall Street would not be an easy decision. Whenever I put money in the stock market, I feel like I am moving from solid ground onto a snow-covered glacier where one can break through the snow and fall into a crevasse at any time without warning. Hopefully, reason would tell me to press on because opportunities to buy into the stock market at book value are very few and far between. And besides, at book value the crevasses can't be that deep, or can they? Is there not a rule somewhere that says "At low book values, logically speaking, there can only be shallow crevasses"? At this point to carry out the plan, to switch into stocks, I would have to go on faith that the worst is over. I would have to ignore the biased emotional opinion of the large number of investors who will by then have experienced plunges into crevasses of varying depths.

To get into the stock market at book value, I would have to buy stocks in the face of a big growling bear market like the one in 1974. I would have to swim upstream against the tremendous flow of as many as eight million investors who can be expected to flee the stock market in another really horrific downturn.⁵ Many of these investors, we can assume, would flee to Main Street looking for a safer place for their money and thus create a sellers' market for real estate. I would have to have the nerve to sell a condominium or two to these refugees from Wall Street and at the same time buy some of the stocks they had just dumped at bargain prices.

So you can see that to describe the circumstances under which it might make sense to trade a condominium or two for financial assets, I had to dredge up from the past quite a disastrous scenario for the world of finance. Will we again see hundreds of billions of dollars of financial assets disappear into thin air any time soon? No one knows for sure, but a lot of people do believe that if it happened once or twice, before it can happen again. But regardless of what happens in the future, in 1998 it was hard to imagine a good reason for selling good income-producing condominiums. No one knew for sure in 1998, but now in 2001 we know the answer; yes, billions of dollars did once again disappear into thin air.

Are there any sure signs that something extreme will occur? No, but there are interesting statistics to worry about. In December 1995, the unmanaged Standard & Poor's Composite Index of 500 stocks was valued at 3.9 times book value, and by late 1996 stocks had become so popular that the value of the total stock market was 95% of the underlying economy (that is, the gross national product [GNP]); no wonder some people feel that the stock market is on the edge of a cliff.[6] In 2001 with the benefit of hindsight, we realize that the NASDAQ was on the edge of a cliff and it did go over that cliff. Also, by the way, in 1996 Warren Buffet himself, I heard in the news, indicated that he did not expect Hathaway to continue to have such high returns as had been experienced in the past. And in 1998 it was announced that Buffet had bought up a significant part of the world's total supply of silver. His goal is to get at least a 15% return every year.[7] Maybe silver will help him meet this goal if the stock market lets him down. The early part of the year 2001 proved that Warren Buffet's concerns were justified; the value of his fund went down as well.

SUPERIOR RATES OF RETURN ON INVESTMENT

We cannot compare the dollar amounts we are investing in our few condominiums to the amount Warren Buffett is investing (he has billions), but we can compare the rate of return and the approach to investing. It is possible to have about the same rate of return that Warren Buffett has as a goal and, in some aspects, to follow a similar investment strategy even though the investment vehicles are so different. This just shows you that money can be made in such everyday, common things as Coca-Cola and condominium homes. (By this, I am not suggesting that your condominium will have the advantage of powerful brand-name identification like Coca-Cola; the condominium rental business is more like dealing in a commodity with a special advantage of a unique fixed location and high quality.)

In general, Warren Buffett makes relatively few investments. He invests only in things he understands and stays with those investments for a long time if the investments continue to perform as expected. He is in a much better position to get a good understanding of a large corporation than the average person because he is such a significant investor. He buys millions of shares. He gets to know the chief executive officer (CEO) of the company personally and frequently is elected as a board member of the corporation. He normally does not invest in technology companies because, he says, he cannot understand them well enough.

From my five remaining easy-to-understand condominiums, I expect to ultimately realize a 15% to 20% total return on investment. More than half of this return, I expect, will have come from monthly cash flows when everything is said and done. The rest of the gain, I speculate, will have come from a less predictable and reliable source of profit: appreciation. When and exactly how much profit I will realize from appreciation I don't know for sure because that depends so much on the uncertain future. Of course, early investors in Berkshire Hathaway also will not realize their significant gains from appreciation until they sell their shares (Berkshire Hathaway does not pay dividends). Gains due to appreciation in price, in the stock market as in the real estate market, are subject to market risk until you sell. Cash flow and dividends that you actually receive are real gains that you can spend or put in the bank. And cash flow alone can make a rental condominium a good investment. In about 20 years, cash flow could return to you all the money you originally put into the condominium. Additional gains from appreciation would be icing on the cake.

YOUR CONDOMINIUMS WILL MAKE YOU THINK AND ACT LIKE THE WORLD'S GREATEST INVESTOR

The nature of direct investment in real estate will cause average small investors to invest like Warren Buffett except that they are investing in real estate and not stocks, of course. Stock investments don't cause investors to automatically act like Warren Buffett. Stocks are easy to buy, and it is not difficult to form an opinion about stocks. A vast amount of predigested information about stocks is available. As a result, many people end up doing too much buying and selling. They make buy-and-sell decisions in response to hearsay about the meaning of short-term fluctuations in the stock market.

Real estate, on the other hand, requires you to get information that is specific and unique to the property you are considering to buy as an investment. It is relatively difficult to acquire. And, for most people it is such a large investment that it will dictate a careful long-term approach. To be a good condominium picker, you will have to do more work than most people do in picking stocks. Making sure you only pick the right condominiums is crucial. Unlike stocks, condominiums, once they are in your investment portfolio, cannot usually be sold quickly at a small loss to correct an error in selection. For these reasons, most people will do better investing in real estate.

The notion that real estate can be a superior investment for many people is not just a biased idea originating exclusively from real estate people. Peter Lynch, one of the most successful stock mutual fund managers, also champions such an idea. In one of his books about how to invest in Wall Street, he clearly agrees with the frequently expressed viewpoint that for many people their best investment in the end turns out to be their home. This really does sound like something you might hear a real estate agent say. You might easily dismiss the real estate agent's opinion as self-serving, because she is in the business of selling homes. But it could be a big mistake to discount without a second thought such an opinion about real estate when it comes from one of the most famous and accomplished Wall Street gurus. Think about it: Peter Lynch made billions of dollars by investing in stocks on Wall Street; what interest would he have in misleading you about the value of real estate on Main Street? And it is important to note that when Peter Lynch is considering real estate as an investment in his book, he is not talking about income property but only about gains people might realize from buying and selling their own homes.[8] He does not consider taking that powerful next step of buying more than one home and then renting out the extra ones. Rental income, sometimes the biggest factor in generating gains from real estate, has not been thrown into the equation.

Andrew Tobias, a well-known writer on investing, is appropriately skeptical about making easy money in the stock market. In general, he suggests that no one investment will lead us to riches quickly, but he seems optimistic about saving everywhere we can as a way up for most of us. He also evaluates real estate *investment* in his book, *The Only Investment Guide You'll Ever Need*. Tobias does not go into any detail about how to invest in real estate but does express a general opinion about real estate by stating that "the hand-tailored approach takes a lot more effort; but, done carefully, is less likely to go wrong." This view of real estate only partially applies to my method. The approach in this book is hand tailored, but you don't literally do any work with your hands. It is a method of investing in real estate that takes much less effort than most people would expect any direct investment in real estate to require. And so far, my approach has never really gone wrong. Tobias also reveals that he has a very common idea about what a landlord's life must be like by stating that "real estate, indeed, can be as much a part-time *job*—scouting for properties, arranging their purchase, fixing them up, interviewing tenants, keeping them happy, negotiating the bureaucratic maze, cajoling plumbers in emergencies—as an investment."[9] Your reaction to this realistic description of what landlording can be like for some landlords might be to cross real estate off your list of possible investments. You might even decide that the only sure and safe thing to do is follow all the tips on how to be thrifty provided by Tobias and start furiously saving your way to affluence. But the only parts of Tobias's statement that apply to the method described in this book are that you do have to arrange the purchase of some properties two or three times in your lifetime and that these investments are less likely to go wrong. Someone else takes care of all the other things Tobias is worried about. You delegate the part-time job part to someone else.

I personally know of numerous rental condominium units that have been in the possession of the same owners for a very long time. I have to believe that most of these owners are keeping and renting them out for so long because they are working out well. I don't personally know of anyone who has realized a loss by investing in a few, select condominiums. Most people, I think, could tolerate a significant negative cash flow for only a relatively short time. A few people who have told me how they feel about their rental condominiums indicated that they intend to basically hold onto them, as long as they do not incur any significant losses. It just seems to them like a good idea to have some extra real estate besides their home in their investment portfolio.

NATURALLY A SOLID INVESTMENT

There seems to be something more solid about real estate than the mere numbers that tell you how it is doing as an investment. When you buy stocks from your stock broker, you get only a very thin piece of paper that confirms the purchase. The numbers on the paper tell you how many shares you now own at a given price. When you buy a condominium, true, you get a lot more paper, but you can also go to see and touch something more solid—wood, aluminum, vinyl, stucco, stone, concrete, or brick—than just a piece of paper. You can even go in and get real *shelter.*

A condominium is such a solid thing to buy that a banker will loan you as much as 95% of the money you need to buy the place. Try to go to a banker and get him to lend you 95% of the money you need to buy $100,000 worth of stock shares in Microsoft. This is not to imply that borrowed money is not used to buy stocks. In early 1997 I read that the amount of money borrowed to invest in stocks increased by 16%. This could be another source of instability in the stock market.

But just because something is solid does not mean that it will always be a good investment. Gold, for example, is solid, but it can be a bad investment for long periods of time. Gold provides no cash flow or tax shelter, and you can experience many years of no increases—or even decreases—in the price of gold. During these periods, the phrase "it's as good as gold" is hardly used. But gold will probably always be a better investment than owning a solid condominium in a ghost town. When you invest in an investment-grade condominium, you are not just investing in bricks and mortar or whatever else it might be made of but really in a stream of future earnings.

NOT AN INVESTMENT FAD

What can be more important than shelter? Actually, not much. Wilderness survival training courses instruct you to seek out shelter first and worry about water and food later. But you don't have to be in a survival situation to see the everlasting importance of shelter. Just observe people backpacking in the great outdoors when they get to a campsite late or when the weather is a little threatening; you will usually see them putting up the tent first and only then start working on dinner. And when you are traveling cross-country by car, isn't finding good secure shelter at the end of the day the first and top priority?

EVEN SHELTER IS NOT A GUARANTEE

So if you are dealing in something as essential as shelter, does that mean it will always be a good investment if you keep it long enough? Of course not; shelter, like food, is subject to the forces of supply and demand. Overbuilding could keep rents down (the invisible hand at work again, causing you, the landlord, to provide for the general interest). You could make a big mistake and buy shelter with too many serious flaws at too high a price. Just because something is very essential does not guarantee that you will make money by dealing with it. But shelter, on the other hand, won't become obsolete like typewriters did.

Software and other technological advances may very well take away part of the banking business from the bankers, but it is hard to visualize software that would take from you your condominium rental business. A change in tax laws could affect the ability of your condominium to shelter you from taxes, but the shelter your condominiums provide will never go out of fashion. And as long as your condominium can provide this basic shelter from the elements to your tenants, it will also shelter you from the less obvious effects of inflation in the short run and the long run. The stock market, on the other hand, is usually not a good place to be when there is a lot of inflation, at least not in the short run.

REAL ESTATE OUT OF FAVOR—TIME TO BUY?

There has not been much inflation lately, and the stock market has been a good place to be. More money has been flowing into stocks relative to real estate for a long time now. The stock market, as a result, has had a tremendous increase in price. According to Stephen Leeb, "In 1980 homes were worth twice what stocks were worth. Today, stock values are 25 percent or more ahead of homes. If the stock market should fall mightily, the damage to the system could be enormous."[10] In this sense, real estate has been out of favor for quite a while, and when something is out of favor, that is the time to buy it at a bargain price. Is that not the same kind of advice you get from market timers and value investors in the stock market?

At one time California real estate prices increased by about 15% every year, and extraordinary future expectations were extrapolated from this trend. But finally the pendulum swung back, and prices for residential real estate went down significantly in southern California. According to a federal study, the average house lost 9.6% in price from 1990 to 1995 but then registered a 0.9% average increase in 1995.[11] If this big, general decline in prices has affected lower-priced condominiums, could there be an opportunity to buy a rental condominium in California that would give you an immediate, generous, positive cash flow? And should you not look for an opportunity like that in Utah, where the price for an average home jumped by 11.4% in market resale in 1995? In Washington State, where my condominiums are located, the gain in 1995 house prices was only 4.2%; does that mean I should have been in Oregon, where the gain was 9.1%?[12] Or should I look for condominiums in the real estate hot spots that were acting up in 1996, in middle America? But more recent statistics in 1997 bore good news, and maybe they will allow me to stay put with a clear conscience that I am not missing out on anything. In 1997 local newspapers reported that rents in Seattle would go up 10% in 1997 and by 10% to 15% in 1998 and that apartment prices would go up by 17%. The average per-unit figure for apartments was $40,000 at the beginning of 1996, and at the end of 1996 it was $48,000 (that works out to a 20% increase).[13] This goes to show you don't have to chase statistics like a dog chasing his tail. If you stay put in a good location, the right kind of statistics will chase you down sooner or later. From the perspective of the year 2001 we see that California's real estate prices have recovered (but what will be the effect of the energy crisis?) and in the Seattle area the real estate market, especially for condominiums, has continued to be very strong. I am amazed at the number of new condominium projects popping up all over the place in the Seattle area.

But don't these statistics suggest that the real estate price trends of the 1970s and 1980s have started again? And shouldn't you act quickly to take advantage of this trend? No, you cannot be sure any kind of a price trend has started. You should not make your condominium investment decisions based on apparent swings in the overall real estate market, let alone try to coordinate your investment with what is happening in the stock market. You do not want to be mistaken for one of those people who is trying to get rich quickly by predicting what the national economy will do next. The investment decision should be based mainly on the specific property and the conditions in the local real estate market. Making decisions to buy or not to buy a condominium unit based on national or regional economic statistics about real estate could result in some very bad decisions. For example, the last condominium I purchased (in 1986) has appreciated by about 155% during the last 15 years. Real estate in general has been out of favor relative to many other investments available in the stock market during most of this time period. I could have heeded general statistics and avoided buying more real estate, but if I had done that, I would have paid rent for 15 years and missed the 155% paper gain that my latest condominium has so far experienced. Real estate in general was flat, and the price of one or two of my older condominiums may also have participated in this flatness during the first 10 years of this period, but one particular condominium of mine refused to go along with national trends and continued to appreciate.

According to national statistics, during the 1980s after inflation was conquered, property values sagged and real estate was suffering. My cash flow, however, continued as normal during this period, so can you say my condominiums suffered as well? If the cash flow from my condominiums was supposed to increase during this period but did not because of the general sagging of property values, then you could say that my property suffered as well. But I had not been counting on an increase in cash flow, so if my condominiums' performance did really suffer, I did not feel the pain. If you are not aware that you were supposed to gain more than you did, you don't feel a loss. By all this I am not implying that you can buy a piece of property that will never be noticeably affected adversely by bad times. I am saying that if you own high-quality rental condominiums, it may be difficult for you to detect and measure the impact of moderately bad times in real estate markets upon your properties. In a really bad market for real estate, where the average price of a home actually drops significantly, I would expect the tax assessor to tell me I am losing on paper by reducing the valuation of my condominiums and my property taxes. In 25 years I have yet to see any dips; my condominiums either stay flat or go up. Home prices, based on national statistics, do dip, but they do not dip as much as stock prices, and in many long periods of time they beat stocks in price appreciation. This is why for so many people the home they have owned for 30 to 50 years is their best investment even without renting it out.

The Great Depression caused the biggest dip in house prices. That dip was probably big enough to cause a setback to even the most conservative real estate investment program. But it was a relatively mild dip when compared with what happened to stock prices. And once again, you should note that although gains from rental income are not considered in these statistics, they must have also suffered because I have read stories about how some families in the 1930s moved each year to take advantage of falling rents.[14] The 1930s must have been terrible for landlords; they could not pay off their mortgages with cheaper money due to negative inflation, and they faced falling rents on top of that.

In 1997 and early 1998, people were not talking too much about depression, but there was a lot of talk about deflation. Some economists were suggesting that deflation was actually being imported into this country from Asia. The Asian currencies, they said, were collapsing in value relative to the dollar, and as a result super-cheap imported Asian goods were causing a general price decline, or deflation, in this country. Now deflation is supposed to be bad for everything (including condominiums) except cash. If in 1998 there really were deflation that normal statistics were failing to measure, my condominiums might have also failed to register a negative impact. The net rental income from my condominiums increased by 33% in 1997. If I was actually getting this additional rental income in the form of more valuable or deflated dollars, so much the better.

When I started writing this book in February 1996, I had no idea that when I was finishing it up, my condominiums would be performing at such a high note and that investments in financial assets would be starting to look so shaky. However, if the Asian financial crisis really had spun out of control and turned into a global economic disaster that seriously impacted the real economy, Boeing and Microsoft would also have felt some real pain. There is no getting around it: My condominiums would also probably have felt some of that pain. The well-being of my condominiums depends to some degree upon the disposable income available to people in the Puget Sound area, and Boeing and Microsoft provide a significant part of that disposable income, which helps generate economic growth that tends to reduce vacancy rates and push up rents. A drastic slowdown in the economy, on the other hand, would be bound to have a negative effect on rental income. No one knows what will happen to the economy next year, but I am confident that I will continue to crow about my condominiums' ability to withstand the worst financial and economic turbulence that might hit our region someday. To update you to the year 2001, I can tell you that Microsoft and Boeing have had problems. There is talk of a softening of the economy in Washington state but the real estate market so far is holding up really well. Once again history proves that good real estate is tougher than stocks when faced with a weak economy. See Appendix L for data on how well real estate and especially condominiums have continued to perform in the Puget Sound area of Washington State.

RENT CONTROL: THE VISIBLE HAND

Rent control? Could this be a more terrible man-made disaster for landlords than the Great Depression? Stocks don't have dividend control. I personally have never had to deal with rent control, but I know it can make a landlord shake with anger just talking about it. The angry person in question was my next-door neighbor in my first condominium (the very successful solid high-rise). He told me that he owned a fine condominium in Munich, Germany, and that he was renting it out but was losing money every month (this is where he started to shake) because a combination of rent control regulations and laws designed to protect elderly low-income tenants had trapped him in a lose-lose situation. According to my neighbor, his tenant, a fine old lady, had a complete legal right to continue to occupy his condominium in Munich at very low rent until she decided to move or died.

A very visible hand of the local government had a tight grip on him. It was apparently squeezing hard enough to make the cash flow in the wrong direction—away from my neighbor. The only way to get out of it, he said, would have been to sell at a significant loss.

When I was looking for investments in Riga, Latvia, I learned that tenants in an apartment that had been privatized had the legal right to continue to occupy the place at the previous low rent for seven years (I heard that in some instances tenants could be bought out of the place for a reasonable amount).

There is no sign of it yet, but if I heard that rent control was coming to Seattle, my first reaction would be to panic and sell all the condominiums. The only reason for hanging on would be if I thought that rent control would be reasonable to landlords, that is, that the visible hand would not be clenched into a fist that squeezed all the profit out of my condominiums. I think it would be wishful thinking to expect to ride it out and wait until rent control was lifted. Rent control laws might indeed be reversed some day, but would the long-lasting effects of rent control on my condominiums be reversible? With rent control out of the way, could I then still come out on top by reaping the benefits of the higher rents that rent control ultimately causes? How long would it take the free market to eliminate the artificial shortages of shelter created by rent control? From what I have read about rent control in such places as New York City, I suspect that rent control and its effects may be about as reversible as would be the effect of a giant sinkhole underneath one of my condominiums.

If you live in an area where rent control poses a real danger, do not try to apply this condominium method. It may not work. And even if you could make a profit under rent control, the aggravation may not make it worthwhile.

If I had to move to an area plagued by rent control, I would consider the condominium method of investing to be out the window. I would implement an Investment Plan B, my next best alternative, under which I would invest mostly in electric utility mutual funds and money market funds. Then I would wait forever, if need be, for the stock market to crash down to book value. When and if the stock market did that, I would use a significant part of the money market funds to buy a stock market index fund. I don't think that Investment Plan B would ever replace that sense of security that my condominiums provide, but hopefully it might come close.

Chapter 7

What Next
and How Far Can You Go?

IF FIVE ARE GOOD, WILL TEN BE TWICE AS GOOD?

If I had 10 condominiums instead of 5 and on average they performed about the same as the ones I have now, for 40 minutes of extra work a month on my part I would double my cash flow. In making this hypothetical expansion, I am assuming that the 5 additional condominiums' locations would be such that my current property management firm could handle them all and that my bookkeeping effort would double to about 80 minutes a month (going to a computerized spreadsheet at this point might be worth it). This is a simple formula: Double your condominiums, double your profit. The problem with this scenario is that I jumped over the hard part: acquiring the 5 additional condominiums that would yield a decent positive cash flow. Simple formulas are not always easy to apply quickly.

KEEP FOREVER! BUT EXPAND FOREVER?

For a moment, let us assume that with a little work I was able to apply this simple formula for continually increasing my profits. Should I do it? If I have the ability to frequently and regularly buy investment-grade condominiums, should I continue to expand indefinitely? The answer is probably not, because in the real world there is the danger of overextending financially.

By too rapidly increasing the number of condominiums in your portfolio, you are inevitably exposing yourself to greater financial risk, even if all the additional condominiums are of investment-grade quality. For example, I usually experience a vacancy rate of about 4% (people who want to be more optimistic would call this a 96% occupancy rate), and without any interest expense I get a very decent positive cash flow. A 4% vacancy rate for one condominium would mean it would be vacant for about two weeks every year. If the rent were $600 a month, a 4% vacancy rent would reduce cash flow for the year by about $288 (4% of the annual rent, which is $7,200, or $600 times 12 months). So, say I acquired a large number of additional condominiums using borrowed money (this means I would have to pay interest expense—the price of having leverage) during a period when the workings of the invisible hand did not allow me to increase rents by even a small amount. And then let us further assume that the very same invisible hand permitted the vacancy rate to increase by 1%, to just 5%. Small unfavorable nibbles of this size are very possible occurrences and may not have a very noticeable effect on someone owning a few condominiums outright but could have a very significant unfavorable impact on total income from all sources if multiplied across a large number of leveraged condominium units. Depending upon how many additional condominiums I had just theoretically acquired, these small relative shifts in profit margins in the wrong direction at the wrong time could nudge the condominium portfolio into a negative cash flow situation that is intolerable even in the short run.

What If Appendix A Stared You in the Face

How quickly you can be nudged into a negative cash flow situation can be demonstrated by using the numbers laid out in Appendix A, which come from an actual condominium. They are a realistic estimate of the situation I will face when I consider putting my next condominium up for rent. So let us assume that I bought 11 more good condominiums, like the one depicted in Appendix A, without making any mistakes in the selection and buying process and with the same kind of financing and that they all have the same rent of $1,000 a month. Great—now I have 11 more good condominiums with a relatively small negative cash flow penalty. But now let us further assume that we get that small nudge in the wrong direction and that the average vacancy rate goes to 5% (instead of a 0% vacancy rate); all the positive cash flow of my 5 original, debt-free condominiums would be eaten up. That is all it would take, a 5% shift in the vacancy rate, and suddenly I would have 16 condominiums yielding a total cash flow amount of zero. On top of that, to buy the 11 additional condominiums, I would have to spend $136,323 for the down payments and closing costs (11 × $12,393), which would no longer be in the money fund earning 4% to 5% interest.

Fortunately, the slow and careful unit-by-unit method does not allow you to make a big 11-condominium move like that all at once. To do so all in one fell swoop, you would have to buy an apartment building with 11 apartments in it or one very expensive condominium with performance characteristics like those depicted in Appendix A.

And What about a Marginal Case Like Appendix B?

Now, if the average rent were $1,100 a month and the vacancy rate did not exceed 3%, you could expand with increasing cash flow. Yes, the amount of rent and vacancy rate are important. In a case like that shown in Appendix B, however, the margin of safety is not very great, and you would expand only into situations that provided additional positive cash flow.

100% Vacancy or 0% Occupancy—Does It Scare You?

When you are trying to determine how many condominiums, if any, should be in your investment portfolio, it is worthwhile to contemplate worst-case scenarios. Excluding disasters like fires and earthquakes against which you can insure against but whose ultimate consequences are difficult to calculate, an extremely bad situation for any landlord would be a 100% vacancy rate. For my five rental condominiums, a 100% vacancy rate would mean a yearly $10,136 negative cash flow. A 0% occupancy rate for a condominium like the one depicted in Appendix A would cause an $11,472 negative cash flow—how this is estimated is shown in Appendix G. Because the Appendix A condominium is not debt free, you can see how leverage makes this worst-case scenario even worse. Appendix D shows that a 100% vacancy rate with no leverage would result in a negative cash flow of only $4,128 a year. When things are really bad, it helps not to have any debts.

If my 5 condominiums were appreciating at 3% a year, the amount of this appreciation would roughly offset the negative cash flow that a zero occupancy rate would generate. On paper I would break even—a slightly comforting thought as long as you have the real cash to cover the real negative cash flow. Unlike the case with appreciation, you will never just see it on paper; you will always have to pay for it with money right out of your pocket. The Appendix G rental condominium would have to appreciate by more than 12% a year to offset the negative cash flow that would result if it earned no rental income for one year.

Struck by Lightning During a Shark Attack

In reality, I don't think I will ever experience anything even close to a 100% vacancy rate, not even if we had an outright depression in the local area. In a depression, income available for rent would be drastically reduced. There might be a tremendous outflow of renters from the area. The exodus from Seattle could be like the one experienced during the Boeing bust in the early 1970s or worse. But tenants are real people, and they cannot all disappear into thin air like stock market value. I would automatically compete for the remaining renters by reducing rents as necessary. The strategy is always the same—to maintain my market share by keeping my places as full as possible at all times and under all conditions.

Unless you were unlucky enough to chose a future ghost town as the place to make your investments (if you follow the steps in Chapter 3, such bad luck should not be possible), the probability of no rent at all for a whole year, I suspect, is less than experiencing a setback from a fire or an earthquake. By making this 100% vacancy rate analysis, I am not in any way suggesting that a 20% or even a 10% vacancy rate would be acceptable. If that ever started happening to me, I would know that something was really wrong and start looking into it really carefully to see what kind of corrective action had to be taken. Normally I expect to experience a 4% vacancy rate. A vacancy rate consistently close to zero might mean that rents are too low.

LEAN AND MEAN BREAK-EVEN RATE

My experience indicates that the average income-producing condominium, if it is free of debt, should break even at an occupancy rate of less than 50%. You should never experience a 50% vacancy rate, but it is just good to know that you and your property managers are running an efficient, low-cost operation. In comparison, the average hotel requires a 63% rate of occupancy to break even (based on 1996 statistics).

PORTFOLIO MIX CALIBRATED BY SUCCESS

Ultimately, your investment portfolio will be shaped by decisions you make about your investment objectives, your need for liquidity, your perception of risk, your inflation expectations, and how your various investments perform compared with each other. If you think some condominiums do fit into your portfolio, you should follow the steps outlined in Chapter 3 as closely as possible, because as a small (or even not so small) investor, you cannot afford to make any mistakes when buying something as large as a condominium. How well you do in selecting only good condominiums will probably have a major influence on how big a piece of your investment portfolio will consist of them. About seventeen years ago, my new condominiums were working so well for me that I had the confidence to put 90% of my total investment portfolio into them without worrying much about the lack of balance in my portfolio. Today, my five remaining condominiums are older, but my portfolio is much more balanced. The condominiums represent less than half of my portfolio but are still the biggest source of cash flow. It continues to be a little-work and low-worry portfolio.

ASSETS WITH A REAL FOUNDATION IN YOUR PORTFOLIO

The cash flow from the condominiums flowing into other investments has caused them to become a smaller and smaller part of my total investment portfolio. But I still consider my condominiums to be the most solid part of my permanent portfolio. I do not consider even my investment in a conservative electric utility stock mutual fund to be as solid, because its price fluctuates quite frequently by relatively significant amounts and some expert analysts think that the long-term value of utilities could be adversely affected by major structural changes in the industry that will make the market for electricity more competitive. More competition will force utilities to reduce rates, thus earning less profit. Also, nuclear power generates more risk and uncertainty for investments in utilities. Utilities may continue to grow to be a larger part of my portfolio, because of the automatic reinvestment of dividends, but that does not qualify them to become a permanent foundation for my portfolio like my condominiums. Utilities do not have that hold-forever quality about them anymore. I plan to sell my utility fund if uncertainties about the utility industry increase or if I am presented with an opportunity to sell at an exceptionally high price.

My condominiums, on the other hand, provide consistently good cash flow and protection from inflation, in the short run and in the long run. On top of all that, there is usually some price appreciation that is not induced by general inflation but by economic growth. This extra bonus is a reward for patiently holding onto a good location. And as far as I know, no expert financial analyst has ever written a worrisome article about potential structural changes in the condominium rental industry that could be interpreted as any kind of a threat to the profitable status quo that my rental units enjoy. The foundation for my investments may be getting relatively smaller but remains as solid as ever.

Speculation Versus Cash Flow

The final story of my condominiums is not in and won't be until I sell all of them. Right now I rank my condominiums by cash flow, but when and if I sell them, the sales price may play a role to change the ranking. For example, my waterfront condominium provides an after tax return of only about 5% from rental income, but there are some indications, based on prices of other nearby condominiums for sale, that it could chalk up significant gains when I sell it. These *real* price gains would make up for the relatively deficient cash flow accumulations and thus move it up in the final rankings at the very end of the investment. In other words, I hope my place on the water will behave like a come-from-behind race horse. Indeed, that is speculation. But every investment contains an element of speculation. And my condominiums, sometimes, need the speculative aspect brought out in them; otherwise, they might be completely boring to many people. But this is not the same kind of speculation as that undertaken by a medical doctor in Montana who sent real money, $100,000, to some island off the coast of England. On this island was an expert speculator who apparently promised to turn these dollars from Montana into a much larger sum (and also send it back to Montana at some point, I assume) by shrewdly trading in foreign currencies. There had been a promise of a superior return, but the doctor got a superior loss instead—something close to 100%, as I recall. Hundreds of years of capitalism in this country may not have made everyone immune to the spectacular promises, but at least in most cases the victims seem to know enough about the system to lose quietly (and maybe take only legal action).

People in Latvia, lacking experience with capitalism, held mass demonstrations and picketed the government after they lost their savings to "investment institutions" promising spectacular profits (returns in excess of 90%). In Albania, a violent armed uprising erupted when widespread speculation resulted in a massive wipeout of the life savings of a great number of Albanians. When I speculate about my existing condominiums, I don't send away any fresh new cash anywhere to bet on something that may turn out to be merely a daydream.

Can You Be a Condominium Tycoon, or Is It a Dead End?

This book is mainly about low risk and thinking small. But could this approach serve as a springboard to bigger things? How far can you go with this method? In how many individual condominium units can you invest? Most people I know don't have more than three. I have five, but I read about a man in Florida who owns and successfully rents out 30 individual condominium units. I don't know the details of how he manages them all, but if he does it all himself, he must be one busy fellow. Individual condominium units may not be the ideal vehicle for a really big real estate mogul.

Is there a dead end to this process, say, at 30 or 100 units (there are some pretty nice dead-end streets to be sure), that someone with a big-time talent for real estate investing will run into? Could 100 condominium rental units spread out all over the place be effectively managed? If I had 100 rental units instead of 5, would the only difference be that I would have to do 13 hours of bookkeeping every month instead of 40 minutes? With a hundred units, I suspect, the investment might become a full-time job, but I don't know for sure because so far I have only reached the eight-condominium-and-one-small-house level of experience. However, I imagine that someone who applies this method super successfully might very well want to move on to something more challenging. If they buy one good condominium after another and consistently make money with relative ease but find it too slow and boring, or if they find that 100 individual condominium units all over the place are indeed unmanageable—then this method could feel like a dead end.

They could get around this impasse by taking a completely different road than the one recommended in this book. They could, after gaining sufficient knowledge, start acquiring apartments. With the use of creative financing and tax-free property exchanges, they could move on to bigger properties faster. They could even start selling some properties and then use the proceeds from those sales to get more leverage to buy even more properties. I have heard of these things but have never tried it directly myself, so if you decide to take this faster road, all I can do is to urge you not to underestimate the risk of moving from condominiums to apartments.

Don't forget that on the surface, apartments may appear to be the same type of investment as rental condominiums, but the details of how to actually do it may be different enough that you might be moving out of your area of expertise. There is risk in expanding, even within exactly the same kind of investment or business, so it stands to reason that in moving on to a different business or vehicle for investment, the risk will be even greater. The chance of losing money will increase.

I have talked to some people who are wheeling and dealing all the time in all kinds of large income-producing real estate ventures. They tell me they get into so many deals that they are bound to have many winners and losers in their portfolio at any one time. To continue to be successful, they said, they will have to have more winners than losers—or a few really big winners that more than make up for a lot of small losers. There is no doubt about it: If you can get a "tenbagger" (make 10 times the money you invested) on one deal, you can lose some money on other deals and still get a good investment result. But starting out, how can you be sure you will have any money left before you get that tenbagger? You may be nibbled to death before you bag anything. And with the use of a lot of leverage at the wrong time and place, it is possible for a negative tenbagger to bag *you* before you have had a chance to bag anything at all. When you expand too rapidly or get very large, the don't-ever-lose philosophy is probably out the window. There are numerous examples in business where even large, very experienced companies lose great sums of money by trying to reach beyond their grasp. For example, Boeing tried to move into electronics by forming a new division, and AT&T tried to expand into computers by acquiring another company. Both of these expansion efforts merely ate up profits generated in their primary areas of expertise.

SAME TYPE OF VEHICLE BUT WITH A BIGGER PRICE?

One other possibility, without changing the approach, would be to expand by buying much higher-priced condominiums, providing they yield an equivalent cash flow in terms of percentages. This way, you would not be burdened by a large number of properties, yet you could own much more property in terms of total dollar value. And, of course, the payoff would be a larger cash flow in terms of total dollars. However, the degree of diversification would be reduced, and the price of higher-priced condominiums may not be as stable as middle-class condominiums.

A SLIGHTLY DIFFERENT VEHICLE— CONDOMINIUM HOTEL?

If consolidation and expansion is a goal that you think is worth the additional risk, the vehicles for driving down these very different roads are certainly out there. For example, you could sell all your condominiums and buy one nicely furnished condominium hotel unit in Hawaii for $600,000. Now you would have just one place, and management would be renting it out for you at a rate of $200 a day. But here, too, you may be getting out of your area of expertise. Condominium hotels and resorts are usually nicely set up so that you can easily delegate all the details to on-site management, but how the average cash flow works out might be quite different from how things work with lower-priced residential condominiums. The expenses for a condominium hotel would be quite a bit higher—for furniture, maid service, and more intensive hotel-style management—and this means that even getting $200 every day of the year (you can start playing with these numbers by multiplying $200 by 365 days) would not necessarily make this a good deal at a price of $600,000. As usual, the devil is in the details.

By assuming more and more risk, you could transform yourself from a small-time almost-always-absent landlord to a real entrepreneur (an entrepreneur is one who assumes risk—remember this book is all about *avoiding* risk wherever possible). But this should not be done at the price of your sense of security. After all your work, you do not want to end up in the position of my old dentist. He told me 30 years ago that he had made more than $1,000,000 but was not as happy as he thought he would be when he reached that magical million-dollar mark. He said he could not enjoy himself because he was so afraid of losing it all. I was in no position to give him any helpful suggestions. I probably had a negative net worth at that time, so I could not feel his pain. Also, he had his hands in my mouth and I really was in pain. At that time I did not know enough to tell him to counter his fear by including in his portfolio some stable, moderately priced, income-producing condominiums that are so hard to lose.

Chapter 8

An Act of Faith
Is Still Required

You Bet! The Future Will Be about the Same

You will buy a condominium for investment only if you believe rents will go up enough in the future to maintain your positive cash flow. This means you have faith that expenses such as condominium dues and property taxes will not forever and ever go up faster than the rents you collect. You may at times detect negative trends, but you will know that such trends do not go on and on in a straight line to some illogical, chaotic extreme. You have faith that the forces of supply and demand will quite soon bend the trend line back in your favor. You should be aware of a temporary squeeze on profits, but it is usually not a reason for panic if you have faith in the long run workings of the invisible hand. You also hope and believe that the condominium will increase in value over time—not decrease.

The Past Is Really All You Have to Go On

You need faith because no one has a crystal ball. No one can be sure about what will happen to rents, condominium costs and prices in the future. All you have to go on is what happened in the past. For risky investments, like buying stock options or frozen pork belly futures, the people selling these speculations usually state that past performance is not indicative of the future to protect themselves. So are they asking you to bet your money on what will happen in the future, based on some expert's vision that he magically extrapolated from the chaos of current events? When investing in condominiums, you rely mainly on facts, and all facts come to us from the past. You are not 100% sure, but you have faith that your income-producing condominiums' past performance *is* indicative of the future.

The Strongest Faith Is Not Required

You are going down a well-trodden path for making money. There should be very few surprises. But as to what lies ahead, you will find out for sure only when you get there. The condominium method, however, requires the smallest leap of faith possible. From my experience, the trail gets wider and smoother the further along you go.

You know that in the past, rents and condominium prices have, generally speaking, increased over the long run, so you invest in a condominium with the belief that this trend will continue to apply in the future. You have faith that in the future, market forces of supply and demand will keep the rents and prices for your condominiums ahead of inflation. You have faith that the invisible hand will lift you up comfortably in its palm and not slap you down. But if you do get slapped down temporarily, you will not lose faith in the invisible hand. You will realize it was just probably a wake-up slap. It is not holding you down. You will learn how to more effectively pursue your naked self-interest. The invisible hand will reward you if you are adaptable. All your contribution to the greater good will turn out to be profitable.

The Condominiums Must Sustain Your Faith

Once you have rental condominiums in operation, your faith will have to be justified and reinforced by something you can really believe in—positive cash flow. This faith in condominiums now becomes very conditional and specific. What do you care if rents generally are going up in the country but rents for your condominium, for some reason, are going down? You may still want to believe that the price of your condominium will appreciate in the future, but you will not be able to deny the reality of a persistent negative cash flow. Select your condominiums carefully, or you may lose faith.

I continue to believe in my condominiums because rents have been increasing by about 5% a year on average (this includes the 1991–1995 period that was generally slow for real estate in Seattle). And they have appreciated in value on average by about 6% annually. The final results of the investment, of course, have not been realized and won't be until I have sold them. I won't know how justified my faith in condominiums was until they all are converted back to cash. Theoretically, I could end up selling some units for a lower price than the purchase price. Such a sale would create a real loss. I would have to cover this loss with some of the accumulated cash flow that I thought was all mine to keep all along. Buy high, sell low? This is a common way to lose money in the stock market, but I believe that this will always remain an extremely remote possibility for my condominiums.

On the other hand, I could sell at the peak of a boom in real estate prices and realize a real windfall gain greater than the projected paper gain. However, I don't know when and if I will ever sell, so I don't know if I will ever have a final result for my condominiums. But if I did sell, I believe based on past experience that the result will be a superior return on investment. The two condominiums of mine for which the final results are fully realized—that is, they are history—inspire justifiably great faith. They provided an average return of 36.2% a year. I sold one because it demanded too much attention, but it still gave me a return of 26.7% a year. The other one I sold because it had gone up in price so much, so fast. At that time, I thought it was a good idea to lock in high profits, in this case a return of 45.6% a year, forever and ever. With hindsight, I now realize I should have kept this top performer working for me longer. Over a longer period of time, a rate of return of 45.6% a year probably could not have been sustained, but I probably would be ahead in terms of the total dollar returns. However, regardless of the fact that I might have done better, this is strong evidence to me that I have not been acting on faith alone.

PLACE NO FAITH IN PERSISTENT NEGATIVE CASH FLOW

If you ever actually experience a persistent negative cash flow, you should have absolutely no faith in comforting statements like "You can't go wrong with real estate, they are not making anymore of it. It will always be there for you." This kind of unconditional faith is not a valid reason for buying real estate or holding onto it. I heard about an immigrant in New York who lost his life savings, saved up from years of driving a taxi, by buying some low-rent apartment building—mainly because he had faith and strongly believed that "you could not go wrong by owning a piece of America" (now he probably knows that it also has to be the *right* piece of America at the *right* price). Having a blind faith in slogans like that could put you in the wrong investment and then deter you from taking timely action (like maybe even liquidating a condominium) to stop a debilitating negative cash flow in your investment portfolio. Some people who believe and act on blind faith in real estate per se have even bought remote desert land in Arizona. It may be true that no more land like that is being made and that they own a piece of America and that in 100 years the land will still be there for them. But they won't be there to find out if it is finally yielding any positive cash flow.

Epilogue

A lot has happened in the Seattle area since I completed this book. We had an earthquake, but most structures, including my condominiums, did not sustain significant damage. This was a very impressive reminder that there is no such thing as a risk-free investment. Microsoft is having problems with the government, but nobody knows what that will mean to the local economy if anything at all. Boeing decided to move its headquarters out of Washington State, but most people are not predicting any kind of disaster for Seattle because of this move. I am pretty sure that none of my condominiums has a Boeing headquarters employee as a tenant. Only a thousand people work at Boeing headquarters.

But the really significant news with regard to the subject of my book is how real estate prices and rents have continued to go up and up in very low inflation environment. Also, condominiums continue to become more and more popular; I can see with my own eyes that new condominiums are springing up all over the place. And they continue to go up even though the stock markets have lost trillions of dollars. All these changes in the region have not affected the normal performance of my condominiums except that there have been rent increases and their prices have gone up (quite significantly in some instances). The news about condominiums and real estate seemed to get better after I finished this book. I sometimes felt I wrote my book a couple of years too soon. To rid myself of this feeling, as my work was about to go into production I added Appendix L.

In Appendix L, I included 15 news items about condominiums and real estate that will help reinforce some of the points I make throughout the book even more strongly. These fifteen news items serve to demonstrate that trends in real estate continue to support and validate the ideas laid out in my book. The statistics I provide in Appendix L overwhelmingly refute the bias some people still have against condominiums. However, pay special attention to news item four in Appendix L and what a professor who is a much-respected authority on the stock markets' performance all the way back from 1801 to the present has to say about real estate.

After reading all the statistics, keep in mind that in the future, the stock market will continue to fluctuate in an unpredictable way and that statistics on real estate will also continue to change. But the basic principles on how to invest in condominiums will not change. Chapter 3 instructs you to buy only quality condominiums that can be rented out for a profit. The fundamentals in the method that you should use to seek out and acquire investment-grade condominiums that have everything right with them will constantly stay the same even when the real estate market goes into a slump or starts booming once again. If you apply the method in a disciplined fashion, in some specific locations at certain times you simply may not be able to find a condominium you can buy that meets all the requirements. Do not be frustrated. The method may be saving you from making a big mistake. You can always wait for a better time to buy or find another location to search for just the right property. Taking very carefully thought-out action like that will put real money in your pocket.

Appendix A

Negative Cash Flow but Still Making Money

Price	$94,400
Amount borrowed	$85,500 at 7.75%
Down payment	$ 8,900
Other closing costs	$ 3,493
Amount invested	$12,393

	Monthly ($)	Annually ($)	Percent of Rent	Percent of Expenses
Rent	1,000	12,000		
Property taxes	123	1,476	12.3	28.3
Condominium fee	151	1,812	15.1	34.8
Management	90	1,080	9.0	20.7
Other expenses*	70	840	7.0	16.1
Total operating expenses	434	5,208	43.4	99.9
Net operating income	566	6,792	56.6	130.4
Mortgage payment**	612	7,344	61.2	141.0
Negative cash flow***	46	552		

*Includes maintenance, cleaning, repairs, advertising, and insurance.
**Includes a $77 payment to principle and $535 payment in interest in the monthly payment of $612 at this point. As a result there is total net income of $31 a month.
***Negative cash flow on investment is 4.4% (negative cash flow of $522 divided by the amount of the investment of $12,393 and then multiplied by 100%).

Appendix B

Positive Cash Flow—Rent 10% Higher Than in Appendix A

Price $94,400
Amount borrowed $85,500 at 7.75%
Down payment $ 8,900
Other closing costs $ 3,493
Amount invested $12,393

	Monthly ($)	Annually ($)	Percent of Rent	Percent of Expenses
Rent	1,100	13,200		
Property taxes	123	1,476	11.2	27.8
Condominium fee	151	1,812	13.7	34.1
Management	99	1,188	9.0	22.3
Other expenses*	70	840	6.3	15.8
Total operating expenses	443	5,316	40.3	100.0
Net operating income	657	7,884	59.7	148.3
Mortgage payment**	612	7,344	55.6	138.1
Positive cash flow	45	540		

*Includes maintenance, cleaning, repairs, advertising, and insurance.
**Includes a $77 payment to principle and $535 payment in interest in the monthly payment of $612 at this point. As a result, there is total net income of $122 a month.
***Positive cash flow on investment is 4.3% (positive cash flow of $540 divided by the amount of the investment of $12,393 and then multiplied by 100%).

Appendix C

No Leverage—Same as Appendix A Except No Mortgage Payment

	Price	$94,400		
	Other closing costs	$ 3,493		
	Amount invested	$97,893		

	Monthly ($)	Annually ($)	Percent of Rent	Percent of Expenses
Rent	1,000	12,000		
Property taxes	123	1,476	12.3	28.3
Condominium fee	151	1,812	15.1	34.8
Management	90	1,080	9.0	20.7
Other expenses*	70	840	7.0	16.1
Total operating expenses	434	5,208	43.4	99.9
Net operating income	566	6,792	56.6	130.4
Positive cash flow**	566	6,792		

*Includes maintenance, cleaning, repairs, advertising, and insurance.
**Positive cash flow on investment is 6.9% (the positive cash flow of $6,792 divided by the amount of the investment of $97,893 and then multiplied by 100%).

Appendix D

Worst-Case Scenario without Leverage—Same as Appendix C Except No Rent

Price	$94,400	
Other closing costs	$ 3,493	
Amount invested	$97,893	

	Monthly ($)	Annually ($)	Percent of Expenses
Property taxes	123	1,476	35.7
Condominium fee	151	1,812	43.9
Management	0	0	
Other expenses*	70	840	20.3
Total operating expenses	344	4,128	99.9
Net operating loss	344	4,128	
Negative cash flow**	344	4,128	

*Includes maintenance, cleaning, repairs, advertising, and insurance.
**Negative cash flow on investment is 4.2% (the negative cash flow of $4,128 divided by the amount of the investment of $97,893 and then multiplied by 100%).
To have zero cash flow, you would need to collect about $4,500 of rent for the year. That is about 37.5% of the $12,000 scheduled rent.

Appendix E

Fifty Percent Increase in Rent— with Leverage

Price	$94,400	
Amount borrowed	$85,500 at 7.75%	
Down payment	$ 8,900	
Other closing costs	$ 3,493	
Amount invested	$12,393	

	Monthly ($)	Annually ($)	Percent of Rent	Percent of Expenses
Rent	1,500	18,000		
Property taxes	123	1,476	8.2	25.7
Condominium fee	151	1,812	10.1	31.5
Management	135	1,620	9.0	28.1
Other expenses*	70	840	4.7	14.6
Total operating expenses	479	5,748	32.0	99.9
Net operating income	1,021	12,252	68.1	213.2
Mortgage payment**	612	7,344	40.8	127.8
Positive cash flow***	409	4,908		

*Includes maintenance, cleaning, repairs, advertising, and insurance.
**Includes a $77 payment to principle and $535 payment in interest in the monthly payment of $612 at this point. As a result, there is total net income of $1,098 a month.
***Positive cash flow on amount of investment is 39.6% (the positive cash flow of $4,908, divided by the amount of the investment of $12,393 and then multiplied by 100%).

Appendix F

Fifty Percent Increase in Rent—Same as Appendix E but without Leverage

Price	$94,400
Other closing costs	$ 3,493
Amount invested	$97,893

	Monthly ($)	Annually ($)	Percent of Rent	Percent of Expenses
Rent	1,500	18,000		
Property taxes	123	1,476	8.2	25.7
Condominium fee	151	1,812	10.1	31.5
Management	135	1,620	9.0	28.1
Other expenses*	70	840	4.7	14.6
Total operating expenses	479	5,748	32.0	99.9
Net operating income	1,021	12,252	68.1	213.2
Positive cash flow**	1,021	12,252		

*Includes maintenance, cleaning, repairs, advertising, and insurance.
**Positive cash flow on amount of investment is 12.5% (the positive cash flow of $12,252 divided by the amount of the investment of $97,893 and then multiplied by 100%).

Appendix G

Worst-Case Scenario with Leverage— Same as Appendix A Except No Rent

Price	$94,400	
Amount borrowed	$85,500 at 7.75%	
Down payment	$ 8,900	
Other closing costs	$ 3,493	
Amount invested	$12,393	

	Monthly ($)	Annually ($)	Percent of Expenses
Property taxes	123	1,476	35.7
Condominium fee	151	1,812	43.9
Management			
Other expenses*	70	840	20.3
Total operating expenses	344	4,128	99.9
Net operating loss	344	4,128	100.0
Mortgage payment**	612	7,344	177.9
Negative cash flow***	956	11,472	

*Includes maintenance, cleaning, repairs, advertising, and insurance.
**Includes a $77 payment to principle and $535 payment in interest in the monthly payment of $612 at this point. As a result there is total net loss of $879 a month.
***Negative cash flow on investment is 92.6% (the negative cash flow of $11,472 divided by the amount of the investment of $12,393 and then multiplied by 100%).

Appendix H

King County Home Sales

Year	Average Price ($)	Change (%)
1996	210,693	+4.0
1995	202,639	+3.8
1994	195,296	+5.4
1993	185,272	+1.5
1992	182,542	+2.5
1991	178,146	−0.4
1990	178,838	+26.4
1989	141,484	
Average % increase for seven years		+6.17

Source: *Seattle Post-Intelligencer,* February 28, 1997

Appendix I

Rate of Return on Investment from Rent (Net Income) and Price Appreciation

Condominium Number	1993 (%)	1994 (%)	1995 (%)	1996 (%)	1997 (%)	Total (%)	Average (%)	Appreciation (%)	Total (%)
1	10.0	11.3	12.1	9.8	9.5	52.7	10.5	11.9	22.4
2	Sold in 1981; see calculation of total return in Appendix J.						45.6	6.6	19.6
3	12.8	14.0	11.9	11.2	15.1	65.0	13.0	6.6	16.3
4	11.6	5.5	11.9	7.6	11.9	48.5	9.7		
5	Sold in 1992; see calculation of total return in Appendix K.						26.7		
6	4.3	4.6	5.7	3.2	9.8	27.6	5.5	1.4	6.9
7	2.2	4.4	3.4	4.6	4.8	19.4	3.9	4.2	8.1
*Totals							42.6	30.7	145.6
**Average rate of return from rent								8.5	
**Average appreciation rate								6.1	
**Total average rate of return									20.8

*Includes all seven condominiums.

**Excludes condominiums sold, numbers 2 and 5.

The rates of appreciation included in this chart are based on the calculations presented in Chapter 2.

175

Appendix J

Rate of Return Calculation
for Condominium Number 2

Year	Initial Investment ($)	Return On Investment ($)	Return (%)	Cumulative Return ($)
1976	−5,537			
1977		297	5.4	297
1978		95	1.7	392
1979		277	5.0	669
1980		1,184	21.4	1,853
1981*		3,224	58.2	5,077
1982		2,317	41.8	7,394
1983		2,317	41.8	9,711
1984		2,317	41.8	12,028
1985		18,789	339.3	30,817
Total		30,817	556.4	
Average return		3,082	55.6	

An internal rate of return (IRR) for number 2 would be 26.4%. An interest rate of a little more than 20% compounded annually could give you a similar return. But the calculation for the return on investment used in this book for the purpose of making consistent comparisons to other investments is the following: The $5,537 invested 10 years later has increased to $30,817. This is a total return of 456.6% ($30,817 minus $5,537 divided by $5,537 and then multiplied by 100%). This total return of 456.6% is then divided by 10 years to yield a total average return of 45.6%.

*Condominium number 2 was sold in 1981. Return on investment after the sale comes from sale contract installment payments.

Appendix K

Rate of Return Calculation for Condominium Number 5

Year	Initial Investment ($)	Return On Investment ($)	Return (%)	Cumulative Return ($)
1978	−1,300			
1979		−101	−7.8	−101
1980		925	71.1	824
1981		831	63.9	1,655
1982		677	52.1	2,332
1983		−526	−40.5	1,806
1984		−714	−55.9	1,092
1985		−1,637	−125.9	−545
1986		−1,067	−82.1	−1,612
1987		−579	−44.5	−2,191
1988		−1,462	−112.5	−3,653
1989		−162	−12.5	−3,815
1990		−503	−38.7	−4,318
1991		−338	−26.0	−4,656
1992*		2,337	179.8	−2,319
1993		9,171	705.5	6,852
Total		6,852	526.0	
Average return		428.2	32.9	

An IRR for number 5 would be 12.9%. An interest rate of a little less than 12% compounded annually could give you a similar return. But the calculation for the return on investment used in this book for the purpose of making consistent comparisons to other investments is the following: The $1,300 invested 16 years later has increased to $6,852. This is a total return of 427.1% ($6,852 minus $1,300 divided by $1,300 and then multiplied by 100%). This total return of 427.1% is then divided by 16 years to yield a total average return of 26.7%.

*Condominium number 2 was sold in 1992. Return on investment after the sale comes from sale contract installment payments.

Appendix L

More Recent News
about Condominiums
and Real Estate

Ｎews about condominiums and real estate got better and better after the manuscript for my book was completed. The following is a rundown of some news items I selected along with my comments just before my manuscript went into production:

People who keep telling me that houses increase in value faster than condominiums should understand that that is not always true. How fast property appreciates depends upon a lot of factors. Location, of course, is very important (the saying "location, location, location" applies just as much to condominiums as houses) as are the construction quality of the structure, the condition of the local economy, the supply and demand for shelter, and so on. The following quote indicates that condominiums continue to increase in value very well indeed: "A studio that sold in March of '95 for $80,500 was recently listed at $113,000 and a one-bedroom that sold in January of '97 for $148,500 was just listed at $162,950. All this in the same building—Seattle Heights."[1]

These numbers indicate that the studio increased in value by 40 percent from 1995 to 1998 and the one-bedroom appreciated by 9.7 percent in less than a year—not bad considering what has happened on Wall Street early in 2001.

Next I have a quote about a condominium that performed better still in terms of price appreciation: "Talk about the hot condo market. Units in Belltown Court that were offered in

1996 in the low $100's may now command up to $160,000 with a very short market time."[2]

This statement indicates a 60 percent increase in value. I bet that now some NASDAQ investors wish they had invested in something like Belltown Court instead.

The previous statement is an example of condominiums appreciating over a relatively short period of time, two years. The following quote describes a longer investment period of time, from 1970 to 1998. "Having paid $29,000 for a two bedroom in the initial offering, he is amazed to see recent sales in the complex as high as the mid 150's."[3]

This is good long-run performance for the Bridgehaven Condominium. It increased about five times in value in 28 years. This just goes to show you that condominiums can appreciate over the short run as well as the long run.

The next quote about real estate is one of the most impressive I have read because it does not come from a real estate person or from a magazine dedicated to writing about real estate. Instead, it comes from Jeremy Siegel, a finance professor at the University of Pennsylvania's Wharton School, who also wrote the classic text *Stocks for the Long Run* (McGraw-Hill, 1998). "'In a severe inflationary period, real estate tends to do better than stocks, as the 1970s demonstrated,' [Siegel] says. By contrast, severe inflation would devastate bonds, just as it would stocks."[4]

Elsewhere in this article the professor makes it clear that over a 30-year period, you can expect real estate to outperform stocks and bonds. So for your safety, you should have some real estate, but what about having some gold when there is severe inflation? I bought some gold a very long time ago and that investment has also been in a loss position for a very long time. And gold does not pay any rent. But it is also true that we have had low inflation for a long time. If a high rate of inflation returns, maybe gold will shine once again, but then I will also expect the price increases in my condominiums to at least keep up with that high rate of inflation.

The following is another report in a newspaper about how condominiums are going up in price: "Those buyers who hope to squeeze in by buying one of Seattle's 22,000 condominiums aren't going to find the news much better, Baldwin believes."[5] "That's because just 10 percent of condominium units still sell for under $100,000—mostly studios and one-bedroom units."[6]

Yes indeed, the dynamic forces of supply and demand are bound to have a squeezing effect on someone. Only on a blackboard, where you can see the lines representing supply and demand neatly intersecting, do these powerful economic forces appear to be in equilibrium—and painless.

The following statement suggests that it is wise to try to keep your condominium investments toward the low end: "Supply remains far short of demand in all types of housing and particularly for condos selling at less than $200,000."[7]

I should carry this next quote around and be ready to show it to the next person who tells me that houses appreciate faster than condominiums. This report is clearly telling us that in a specific location and during a specific time period, condominiums appreciated faster than houses by 5.5 percent (doing the math on the quoted 18 percent minus 12.5 percent): "In King County, the median price of single-family homes jumped nearly 12.5 percent from October 1998 to $242,250 last month. The median condo price shot up almost 18 percent during the same year to $155,750."[8]

Next is another report (admittedly from a magazine dedicated to condominiums) about another pretty hefty price increase in a condominium in one year: "At that time [1997] we were predicting at least a four-year hold to compensate for cost of sale, but 10–20% increases in price made resale with profit possible in the space of one year."[9]

Over the long run it would not be reasonable to count on such large price increases year in and year out without a pause or slowdown. The expectation of a four-year hold was a reasonable prediction. This time perhaps they were a little lucky.

The following statement again alludes to what I wrote about earlier in this book. Markets for condominiums and houses are connected. The forces of supply and demand cannot be neatly fenced in when there are people out there seeking good-quality shelter for the best price possible: "High house prices spilled over to condominiums. . . . Throughout much of 1998, the median price of a King County condo was in the $120,000–$130,000 range. Throughout last year it climbed in November reaching $152,000."[10]

This next quote suggests that there will be many more condominiums in our future and that there will be room for more people to get into the type of investing described in this book without creating a bad investment environment where condominium projects have too many renters: "Multifamily building sprees have happened before, such as during a Boeing expansion in the late 1980s. But most of those dwellings were apartments designed for short-term living. In the latest cycle, roughly half the new multifamily dwellings are owner-occupied condos, indicating a profound change in housing choices."[11]

If Mike Lindblom is correct and a "profound change in housing choices" is occurring, then this is profoundly good news for condominium investors.

The following quote once again emphasizes the wisdom of trying to keep your condominium investment portfolio in lower-priced condominiums: "What about the impact of a stock market bust on home values below the super-luxury category in high-tech-driven local economies? It's likely to be little or nothing, unless employers begin laying off large numbers of workers."[12]

Here we go again . . . another quote I should carry around with me to show to people with a bias against condominiums' price appreciation potential: "Seattle home prices have jumped 27.5 percent in two years (1998 and 1999). Seattle condominiums have climbed even faster. The median sales price in the past 12 months was $186,250, up 33 percent in the past two years."[13]

Thus, in two years condominiums went up in price faster than houses by 5.5 percent (33 percent minus 27.5). If this keeps going, price increases in the condominium market will spill over into the house market, and condominiums will pull up the price of houses.

The next quote describes how condominiums are establishing themselves in a big way in downtown Seattle: "Big condo and apartment complexes—those of more than 100 units— accounted for more than half of the housing growth, with 37 percent of the units slated for the greater downtown area."[14]

"The condos advertise for between $158,000 for a studio to $800,000 for some two-bedroom units."[15]

It is all well and good that Seattle is developing a very lively downtown, but as far as investing in the condominiums there, they are too far up on the high end for me. Think about it. Could you get a rent of $1,600 for that $158,000 studio, let alone $8,000 for a two-bedroom unit? Remember that the stock market has recently been in bear territory and that many people are feeling less wealthy. And some, I am sure, actually *are* in fact less wealthy. Now fewer people will be around who are willing, ready, and able to pay such high rents.

The following statement reinforces what I wrote about earlier in my book: It is not unusual that a part of your condominiums' price increases will actually reflect real gains. Many times your condominiums will provide you with a bonus above and beyond mere protection from inflation: "Today, inflation, as measured by the Consumer Price Index, is not a motivating factor in home buying. Inflation in the economy overall has been below 3 percent for half a decade. Housing values, by contrast, have been inflating by 4 percent to 8 percent."[16]

The next quote can be taken as proof that the markets for condominiums and houses are very much connected. The statistician apparently recognized the unity of this real estate market and has lumped condominiums and houses together under one statistical number for both types of properties. He may have said to himself: "Shelter is shelter. What difference does it make when all I want to do is provide the public with the latest median price of shelter in King County and Snohomish County?"

"The median price for homes and condos in King County was $230,000, up from $225,000 the same month a year ago. In Snohomish County, the median price was $201,000, up from $181,575 the same month a year ago."[17]

This statistic simply tells you that the median price of residential property that people buy (condominiums and houses) went up by a certain amount in one year (even taking the earthquake into account). This is good background information, but it will not help you buy a good investment-grade condominium. For help in that department go back to Chapter 3.

Glossary

AMORTIZATION

Amortization is the repayment of borrowed money. For example, in Appendix A, the monthly mortgage payment of $612 includes a $77 payment to principle and a $535 payment to interest. The $77 is that month's repayment of borrowed money and is not an expense that reduces total net income, but it is an outflow of cash that reduces cash flow.

CASH FLOW

Imagining a business or investment without cash flow is like trying to imagine an animal without blood; neither could exist without internal fluids that bring them to life. Your goal is to tap some of this life-giving fluid for yourself on a regular basis. Positive cash flow should be a fundamental requirement for which you always look, just as a good rock-climbing technique requires you to look down at your feet frequently to make sure your footing is firm and that you are properly balanced.

Cash flow is the net amount of cash you actually receive that you can keep, spend, or invest. For cash flow to be a meaningful indicator of sustainability, it should usually come from continuing operations (rent) and not from the sale of productive assets (a condominium). In terms of income or earnings (not counting depreciation), you will normally be doing better than in terms of cash flow. By focusing on positive cash flow as a requirement, you will give yourself an extra margin of safety. You are less likely to kid yourself about the amount of cash you have received than about some projections into the future. Estimated gains from price appreciation or from a tax shelter effect may not come true in the future. Stable and regular cash flow is something you can really count—and count on.

COMPLICATIONS OF DEBT AND TAXES

If you did not use borrowed money to buy your condominiums, you would not have to concern yourself with leverage and amortization because you would not have either; cash flow could be easily defined as being the same as net operating income. Also, if you decided not to take advantage of all the tax shelter that is available, you could forget about calculating depreciation as well. I know only one person who does not depreciate his rental property; apparently he prefers to pay his taxes sooner rather than later. And I understand from talking to tax lawyers and a CPA that when he sells the property, the IRS will calculate depreciation for him because he "should have done it."

But because most of you will borrow money to buy real estate and will think it is wise to reduce current income taxes, you will have to get an understanding of these terms. Even a straightforward investment such as rental condominiums gets a little more complicated when you get involved with finance and income taxes.

DEPRECIATION

Depreciation is an accounting expense, caused by loss of value from the use of the condominium that allows you to reduce the amount of income taxes you have to pay every year. You leave this calculation to your tax accountant. She will calculate the amount of depreciation that you can subtract from your taxable income for each condominium. At tax time your taxable income will be lower, and the amount of income taxes you have to pay will be reduced thanks to your condominiums.

For example, one of my condominiums has a depreciation expense of $4,000 every year. This reduces my taxable income by $4,000. At a marginal income tax rate of 28%, my income tax bill would be reduced by $1,120 ($4,000 multiplied by 28%) because of this.

This does not mean that your condominiums will necessarily reduce your total income tax bill, because your total net income may be too large for depreciation expense to shelter all of it.

Also, it is important to remember that the income tax reduction you get because of depreciation is not forever unless you keep your condominiums forever or make the right kind of property exchange. They are not permanent reductions; you have only deferred the payment of these taxes to the future. When you sell the condominium, you will have to pay these deferred income taxes on top of any capital gains taxes.

INTERNAL RATE OF RETURN (IRR)

The discount rate that equates the present value of future cash flows to the cost of the of an investment.

INVISIBLE HAND

The idea that the market forces of supply and demand will cause you to provide for the general interest while you are pursuing your *self*-interest.

LEVERAGE

Leverage means you are using borrowed money to multiply or magnify the gain (or loss) on your investment. For example, if your total investment in a $100,000 condominium is a $10,000 down payment because you borrowed the other $90,000 to buy it and if you then had a $5,000 gain (from rental income or appreciation) from that condominium, this gain would amount to a 50% return on your investment of $10,000 ($5,000 divided by $10,000 multiplied by 100%).

Appendix E depicts a rental condominium where leverage magnifies the positive cash flow gain from rental income. Positive cash flow is $4,908, or 39.6% of the amount invested ($12,393).

Appendix A depicts a rental condominium where leverage creates a negative cash flow. Negative cash flow is $522, or 4.4% of the amount invested ($12,393). See **no leverage** further on in this glossary for a more conservative alternative to taking on any debt at all.

LEVERAGE FOR GAIN, NOT PAIN

Do you always want more magnifying power? No! If the gains from your investment are not large enough to cover the cost of borrowing that money (loan fees and interest expense that you have to pay to get the loan), you will by definition have a total net loss. And, of course, leverage will magnify the percentage rate of that loss just as effectively as it magnifies gains.

So, if you plan to borrow $1,000,000 for nothing down— you can hope and plan on small miracles to illustrate a point, but do not count on them in real life—to buy some property that is going to increase in value by 15% in one year, make sure you are absolutely right about the valuation of the property. Some get-rich-quick real estate courses advertised on television claim that beginners can make money from almost nothing after listening to a few instructional cassettes. This sounds too good to be true, even after you hear a few people on television say they did it, at least once, successfully.

No Leverage

If you did not use borrowed money and bought the $100,000 condominium for cash, you would have no leverage. Without leverage you would calculate the $5,000 gain as only a return of 5% on your investment of $100,000 ($5,000 divided by $100,000 multiplied by 100%). You do not have the magnifying power of leverage.

Appendix F depicts the same condominium as the one shown in Appendix E except that the mortgage has been paid off. There is no leverage. Positive cash flow is $12,252, or 12.5% of the amount invested ($97,893). In this case, the cash flow is much greater in terms of total dollars, but the rate of cash flow return on the amount invested is less than in Appendix E, where you have leverage.

Appendix C depicts the same situation as in Appendix A except that there is no leverage. Without leverage, the cash flow changes from a negative $552 to a positive $6,792. The $6,792 positive cash flow would represent a return of 6.9% on an investment of $97,893.

Endnotes

CHAPTER 2

1. Net income, $1,774, divided by the down payment, $3,190, multiplied by 100%.
2. Based on a five-year average (1993–1996) of net income before depreciation and taxes. See Appendix I for these calculations.
3. $119,000 minus $31,900, divided by $31,900, and then multiplied by 100%.
4. See endnote 2.
5. Amount of total appreciation, 273.0%, divided by 23, the number of years the property has been in my possession (1975 to 1997).
6. Robert A. Rosenblatt, "Economic Numbers Continue to Worsen." *The Seattle Times,* July 7, 2001, A1.
7. $42,500 minus $23,950, divided by $23,950, and then multiplied by 100%.
8. This calculation is made in Appendix J. It is based on the actual cash flows I received over the life of the investment.
9. See endnote 2.
10. $60,000 minus $25,950, divided by $25,950, and then multiplied by 100%.
11. Amount of total appreciation, 131.2%, divided by 20, the number of years the property has been in my possession (1978 to 1997).

12. See endnote 2.
13. $63,000 minus $27,950, divided by $27,950, and then multiplied by 100%.
14. Amount of total appreciation, 125.4%, divided by 19, the number of years the property has been in my possession (1979 to 1997).
15. $26,500 minus $19,950, divided by $19,950, and then multiplied by 100%.
16. This calculation is made in Appendix K. It is based on the actual cash flows I received over the life of the investment.
17. See endnote 2.
18. $39,000 minus $31,000, divided by $31,000, and then multiplied by 100%.
19. Amount of total appreciation, 25.8%, divided by 19, the number of years the property has been in my possession (1979 to 1997).
20. See endnote 2.
21. $140,000 minus $79,000 and $11,500 (special assessment), divided by $79,000, and then multiplied by 100%.
22. Amount of total appreciation, 62.6%, divided by 15, the number of years the property has been in my possession (1983 to 1997).
23. Based on an average of the results from the four nonconversion condominiums described in Chapter 2: Add the percentage gains for condominiums Number 1 (22.4%), 2 (45.6%), 3 (19.6%), and 4 (16.3%) to get a total (103.9%) and then divide this total by 4 to get the average annual gain (26.0%).

CHAPTER 3

1. My sample contained a total of four condominium projects, and the total number of units in each project compared with the number of rental units was the following: Project one, 18 units total, with 4 rental units (22%); project two, 20 total units, with 3 rental units (15%); project three, 20 units total, with 2 rental units (10%); and project four, 88 total units, with 34 rental units (39%). The average of 22%, 15%, 10%, and 39% is 21.5%, but the total number of units for all four projects is 146, and the total number of rental units for all four projects is 43, or 29.4%.
2. Susan Gilmore, "Vertical Growth." *The Seattle Times Magazine,* December 14, 1997, 20–32.
3. Peter Lynch, *One Up on Wall Street* (New York: Penguin Books, 1990), 240.

CHAPTER 4

1. William H. Pivar, *Real Estate Investing from A to Z* (New York: IRWIN Professional Publishing, 1993), 20.
2. Ibid.

CHAPTER 5

1. According to the 1990 U.S. Census, there were 102,263,921 housing units in the United States, and of these 4,847,921 (4.7%) were condominiums; according to U.S. Bureau of the Census's Current Construction Reports, another 334,000 condominiums were built from 1991 to 1995. This adds up to a total of 5,181,921 condominiums. Based on a very small sample of condominium projects and landlords in the Puget Sound area, I estimated that about 30% (see n. 1 in Chapter 3) of all condominium units are occupied by renters and that the average landlord owns about 2 condominium rental units. Using these statistics and my very rough estimates, I made the following calculations: Thirty percent times the total number of condominiums, 5.2 million, gives you 1.6 million condominium rental units, and 1.6 million rental units divided by 2 gives you 800,000 condominium landlords.
2. Leigh Robinson, *Landlording* (El Cerrito, CA: ExPress, 1995), 5.
3. Peter G. Miller, *Successful Real Estate Investing* (New York: Harper-Collins, 1994), 142.
4. Milt Tanzer, *Real Estate Investments and How to Make Them Pay* (Paramus, N.J.: Prentice-Hall, 1996), 30.
5. John Wesley English and Gray Emerson Cardiff, *The Coming Real Estate Crash* (New Rochelle, NY: Arlington House Publishers, 1979), 45.
6. David Volk, "King County Warming Up to Condos." *Puget Sound Business Journal*, February 21–27, 1997, 24.
7. See endnote 1 in Chapter 5.
8. Bill Virgin, "High Home Prices Spoiling American Dream for Many," *Seattle Post-Intelligencer*, October 15, 1997, A11.
9. June Flecher, "Consider a Condo for the Class of 2000," *Wall Street Journal*, August 30, 1996, B6.
10. Dow Jones Real Estate Index, Wall Street Journal, September 6, 1996.

CHAPTER 6

1. Based on an average of the results from the seven condominiums described in Chapter 2: Add the percentage gains for condominiums Number 1 (21.4%), 2 (45.6%), 3 (19.1%), 4 (15.8%), 5 (26.7%), 6 (5.7%), and 7 (7.9%) to get a total (142.2%) and then divide this total by 7 to get the average annual gain (20.3%). To stay on the conservative side and for the sake of simplicity, gains from interest earned on accumulated cash flow are not included.
2. Bill Virgin, "High Home Prices Spoiling American Dream for Many," *Seattle Post-Intelligencer,* October 15, 1997, pg. A11.
3. Benjamin Graham, David Dodd, and Sidney Cottle, *Security Analysis,* 4th ed. (New York: McGraw-Hill, 1962), 592.
4. Jonathan Clements, "Yes, Stock Mutual Funds are Attractive but Don't Abandon Individual Stocks," *Wall Street Journal,* September 24, 1996, C1.
5. In 1970, according to a New York Stock Exchange census, 30 million Americans owned stock, but in 1975 the number had decreased to 25 million, a 16% decrease. And according to *Information Please Almanac Atlas & Year Book,* 50th ed. (Boston & New York: Houghton Mifflin), 59, in 1992 more than 51 million Americans owned stock—16% of 51 million is about 8 million.
6. Arthur Zeikel, "Portfolio Summary," *Merrill Lynch Capital Fund Inc.,* December 31, 1995, 2.
7. Robert G. Hagstrom, Jr., *The Warren Buffett Way* (New York: John Wiley & Sons, 1995), 26.
8. Peter Lynch, *One Up on Wall Street* (New York: Penguin Books, 1990), 68.
9. Andrew Tobias, *The Only Investment Guide You'll Ever Need* (New York: Bantam Books, 1979), 142.
10. Greg Heberlein, "When You're Riding in a Plane That Can't Land, There's No Getting Off," *The Seattle Times,* September 28, 1997, F1.
11. Kenneth R. Harney, "Middle America Is Hot Spot for Real-Estate Appreciation," *The Seattle Times,* September 22, 1996, G2.
12. Ibid.
13. Journal Staff, "Apartment Prices Jumped 17% in '96," *Seattle Daily Journal of Commerce,* December 17, 1996, 1.
14. Roger Lowenstein, "Inflation Bonds: Revere, Rubin & Leather," *Wall Street Journal,* October 3, 1996, C1.

APPENDIX L

1. "Go Downtown . . . " *Condominium Life Styles,* Spring 1998, 16.
2. "Belltown Court: Urban Oasis . . . " *Condominium Life Styles,* Fall 1998, 16.
3. "Bridgehaven: A Sense of Community," *Condominium Life Styles,* Winter 1998, 1.
4. Jonathan Clements, "Investing Isn't Just 'Happily Ever After'," *The Wall Street Journal,* March 2, 1999, C1.
5. Elizabeth Rhodes, "The Big Squeeze: Seattle's Skyrocketing Real-Estate Values Redefining Who Can Live Here," *The Seattle Times,* March 7, 1999, 1F.
6. Ibid., 3F.
7. Joe Nabbefeld, "Condominium Demand Reaches New Maximum," *Puget Sound Business Journal,* April 16–22, 1999, 12.
8. Journal staff, "Condo Prices Take a Big Jump in Area," *Seattle Daily Journal of Commerce,* November 10, 1999, 1.
9. "CLS Takes a Look at the Future of Condominiums in Puget Sound Region," *Condominium Life Styles,* Winter 1999, 21.
10. Elizabeth Rhodes, "Cooling Trend Forecast for Housing Market," *The Seattle Times,* January 2, 2000, G2.
11. Mike Lindblom, "Housing: We're growing closer; Growth law promotes 'infilling' of suburbs," *The Seattle Times,* January 4, 2000, A5.
12. Kenneth Harney, "Will Stock-Market Gyrations Affect Real Estate Market?" *The Seattle Times,* April 23, 2000, F2.
13. Mike Scott, "Apartment Sales Down but Prices Aren't," *Daily Journal of Commerce,* Seattle, April 28, 2000, 3.
14. Jim Brunner, "Housing Boom Sets a Record in Seattle: Downtown Leads the Pack for New-Home Construction," *The Seattle Times,* February 24, 2001, A1.
15. Ibid.
16. Kenneth R. Harney, "Appreciation Decline Appears Uncertain," *The Seattle Times,* March 4, 2001, G8.
17. Luke Timmerman, "Home Sales Keep Rising; Quake Effects Discounted: Low Interest Rates Cited by Brokers," *The Seattle Times,* March 9, 2001, C3.

Index